HOW DO I DO THIS?

The Real and Raw Truth about
Raising a Child with Special Needs

Interviews with Parents

MEREDITH SWIFT

© 2020 Meredith Swift

The content, formatting and design of this book may not in any way be emulated, reproduced, duplicated, or copied in any manner without prior written permission from the publisher.

Created in the Commonwealth of Australia.

All Scriptures taken from the Holy Bible, New International Version, Copyright 2011-2018, by Biblica, Inc. Used by permission. All rights reserved worldwide.

Cover Design by germancreative@Fiverr
Formatted by Jen Henderson @Wild Words Formatting

ISBN: 9780648507338

DEDICATION

To my precious daughters. Always and forever,
I will be thankful God gave you to me.

To all those parents who have been entrusted with the gift of a special needs child. Know that you are never alone—there are many parents who are journeying on the same road that you are on. Your love and your willingness to do what it takes make all the difference in the life of your child.

To my Lord Jesus Christ, who walks beside me every day, helping me to find the joy in all circumstances.

Jeremiah 29:11 *"For I know the plans I have for you," declares the LORD, "plans to prosper you and not to harm you, plans to give you hope and a future.*

Psalm 139:13 *For You created my inmost being,*
You knit me together in my mother's womb.
14 I praise You because I am fearfully and wonderfully made.
Your works are wonderful,
I know that full well.
15 My frame was not hidden from You
When I was made in the secret place,
When I was woven together in the depths of the earth.
16 Your eyes saw my unformed body,
All the days ordained for me were written Your Book
Before one of them came to be.

THANK YOU FOR READING MY BOOK!

You can visit my website and read my blog at:
https://www.meredithswift.org

PLEASE LEAVE A REVIEW

I really appreciate all of your feedback, and I love hearing what you have to say.

Please leave me a helpful review on Amazon or Goodreads letting me know what you thought of the book. Each review is worth its weight in gold. I would be so grateful if you could do this!

TABLE OF CONTENTS

Introduction	1

AGE GROUP 7-12

Sabine and Bobby (Australia)	7
Diana, Scott, Rachel, David, Sadie and Becca (USA)	30
Marta, Tan and Diego (United Kingdom)	41
Francesca and Nathan (Australia)	49
Tulika, Ravish and Vedant (USA)	59

AGE GROUP 13-19

Janine and Andrew (USA)	69
Lisa, John and Mark (Australia)	79

AGE GROUP 20-30

Diane, Jerry, Lena, Ian and Jolene (USA)	93
Ruth and Emily (Australia)	108
Teresa, Graeme, Joseph and Sarah (Australia)	121
William, Sandra and Nowell (Australia)	139
Deborah, Colin, Ryan and Andrew (UK)	148
Gabriella and Jordan (Australia)	158
Meredith and Sarah (Australia)	168

AGE GROUP 30-50

Lucy and Monica (Australia)	195
Sue and Christopher (Australia)	208
Cathy and Lily (Australia)	225
Lilian and Melissa (Australia)	233

FAMILIES WITH MORE THAN ONE CHILD WITH SPECIAL NEEDS

Zoe, Louise, Harry and Tiger (Australia)	249
Ann, Jane and Valen (Australia)	262
April, Scott, Kellis, Garrett, Isaac, Margaret, Virginia, Marianne, Rhetten, April and Scott (USA)	269
Amy, Jeremy, Austin and Andrew (USA)	280
Conclusion	287
Acknowledgements and Thanks	293

INTRODUCTION

The idea for this book was suggested by my dear friend Lisa after we had a long conversation about the challenges we have faced raising our children. We were lamenting the fact that there was no guidebook or manual to tell us exactly what raising a child with special needs entails—only by talking with other parents do we find out the truth of this type of situation. Lisa asked me whether I would consider writing a book which addressed some of what parents of children with special needs face.

I had been meaning to write my daughter Sarah's life story, but I was just not ready yet. Interviewing parents—and being able to tell some of my own experience—was an idea which excited and encouraged me. I knew many parents both locally and from different countries in the world—thanks to Facebook and my own personal networks—who I believed might like to participate. I reached out to these parents and 22 agreed to participate. Their children (and adult children) ranged in ages from 7 right up to 47.

The aim of this book is to be a support and a resource—a road map if you like—for other parents who are journeying the road of having a child (or children) with special needs. I have found that by reading about the experiences of others that I realise I am not alone. The aim of this book is to help other parents realise they are not alone; that there is support, information, encouragement and help available. I wanted this book to be an honest account—no holds barred—of what it means to raise a special needs child. I believe this has been achieved.

I asked each participant the following questions:

HOW DO I DO THIS?

1. Introduce yourself, your family, and your child/children. Include their age, the nature of their special needs, where in the world you live and anything else you can think of that might be relevant. Include a family photo if you wish.

2. Was it always apparent to you that your child had special needs? If not, when did you notice that something was "different" about your child?

3. If you have received a formal diagnosis for your child's special needs, when did this happen? Do you remember what feelings you experienced at the time and was the diagnosis a hard thing to come to terms with? Have you come to terms with it?

4. Did you research about how to help your child? What did you do? Which organisations/professionals did you reach out to?

5. What therapies did/do you use? What routines do you find helpful for your child?

6. How has having a child with special needs affected your family? Your marriage? Your other children, if you have them?

7. How do you take care of yourself? What self-care strategies do you use and how have you been able to implement them?

8. Do you have a faith? If so, how has this helped you cope with life with your child?

9. How important/necessary is your family support or the support of your friends/networks? Do you feel as though you have enough support?

10. What do you hope/think the future holds for your child? Their living arrangements? A job? Marriage and children of their own?

INTRODUCTION

11. What are/have been the joys of raising your child?

12. What are/have been the hardest challenges raising your child?

13. What has your child taught you?

14. How do you view your child's special needs?

15. What would you say to other parents of special needs children just beginning their journey? What advice/suggestions would you have for them?

16. If you could think of one word to describe being a parent of a child with special needs what would it be?

17. Any final thoughts?

18. Please list any organisations in your country that you have found helpful.

Some parents chose not to answer all the questions, and that was okay.

Opening their hearts and minds and the lives of their families was a big ask, but all these wonderful people came through with flying colours.

The result is a book that I believe is a worthy resource for all special needs families—and those who want to understand a little of what it is like to live in this situation.

These are true stories from real parents from all over the world. These are raw and real stories, woven together with threads of heartbreak and hope, grief and joy, courage and fear, tenacity and persistence and deep, abiding love.

AGE GROUP 7-12

- Sabine and Bobby, 7 (autism, generalised anxiety disorder, sensory processing disorder and auditory processing disorder), Australia

- Scott, Rachel, David, Sadie and Becca, 9 (autism), USA

- Marta, Tan and Diego, 9 (autism), United Kingdom

- Francesca and Nathan, 11 (autism), Australia

- Tulika, Ravish and Vedant, 11 (autism), USA

SABINE AND BOBBY (AUSTRALIA)

Introduction:

My name is Sabine and I am a single parent of my 7-year-old son Bobby. We live in Sydney, Australia. My son has Autism Spectrum Disorder, Generalised Anxiety Disorder, Sensory Processing Disorder and Auditory Processing Disorder. It is his autism which is considered a "disability".

Was it always apparent to you that your child had special needs? If not, when did you notice that something was "different" about your child?

When Bobby was around 18 months to two years, I thought he was just a very bright child—memorising the alphabet, colours, shapes, and numbers; and knowing his home address and my mobile number—but he had no other language beyond this. His fixed interest was logos, and he would spend most of his time flicking through magazines looking for them.

My cousin expressed concerns about how I could possibly think this was normal behaviour. Somewhere deep inside of me I knew she was right, but I had no other children to compare Bobby to. I did not see that, even though he knew words, he made no effort to talk to others. When a friend's child commented that "He doesn't talk", I was gobsmacked and defensive. Bobby also lacked real play skills and would not engage with other children. These were signs that all was not right, but I ignored them through fear and some denial that anything could be wrong. When I had my son, I never imagined that he would be anything other than a healthy and happy little boy. I took so much for granted.

For me, autism was a foreign concept I knew nothing about. I took Bobby to our GP, who told me her own son had lined up video tapes when he was young and "He had turned out fine". She reassured me Bobby would grow out of this repetitive behaviour and, lulled into a false sense of security, I pushed down the worry brewing deep within me.

At two-and-a-half years of age, I enrolled Bobby in childcare. From what I now understand, Bobby had so much anxiety separating from me that it acted as a trigger for many things—for example, he would wander around the other children in a circle, completely in his own world, not playing or interacting with them. The staff said he was fine but in reality, he was trying to block the other children out. He was shutting down and retreating into his own world just to cope. I later discovered this is common for children with autism. One day when I picked him up, I got down on my knees to say "Hello" and he just looked straight through me, like I was a stranger. It was chilling. He began to flap his arms when scared and cover his ears to loud sounds. When I googled "flap arms and cover ears" it came back with "autism". I called Bobby's paediatrician, who (luckily) answered the phone. When I told her some of my concerns, she organised to see us the following week.

AGE GROUP 7-12

If you have received a formal diagnosis for your child's special needs, when did this happen? Do you remember what feelings you experienced at the time and was the diagnosis a hard thing to come to terms with? Have you come to terms with it?

Bobby was observed over two sessions with his paediatrician and, on 13 August 2015—one month before his third birthday—he was officially diagnosed with Autism Spectrum Disorder. As part of the diagnosis, I was given the Childhood Autism Rating Scale (CARS) document, which listed 15 categories, each with a scale from 1-4 where you rated your child. It was probably one of the hardest forms I have ever filled in; I did not want to think of my child as just a form that he was to be ranked by. I must have changed the scores over 100 times, trying desperately to rank Bobby in the section that said "Non-Autistic". Instead, I scored him 30.5 which had him sit in the "Mildly-Moderately Autistic" category; our paediatrician scored Bobby at 33. I did my best with this, but looking back, it is clear to me I was clueless.

I vowed I was not going to have my son defined by a diagnosis and a label but my paediatrician told me that without an "official" diagnosis, I would not receive any funding to access the early intervention Bobby needed—and I would struggle to afford the therapy he required. I told her I did not care, and I would find some way to afford it. I was so desperate to avoid a diagnosis. She explained to me that there is a short window of opportunity for early intervention—before five years of age, while the brain is still plastic and can be changed. In fear and panic, I accepted a diagnosis, but the traits of autism were not really explained to me. Because it is a spectrum, every child is different and there are so many layers to it. I was just told to get a bit of speech and occupational therapy—the sooner, the better—and Bobby would be fine. As we left, it still did not register that my son had Autism Spectrum Disorder. I was in shock and denial.

HOW DO I DO THIS?

I really struggled after the diagnosis, sinking into such grief and loss. All the hopes and dreams I had for my son's future seemed to just fly out the window and were replaced with overwhelming fear and worry for what lay ahead. Would he be able to go to school and university, get a job, and marry one day? Would he talk properly? I had such little understanding and I did not know what to expect. There were days when I felt like I was gasping for breath, as though someone had winded me. Experiencing much guilt and blame, I questioned "Why Bobby?" "What did we do to deserve this?" and "What did I do to make this happen?" I would often watch my son, looking for the signs of his autism. When I saw them, I would just sit and cry—many times I sobbed myself to sleep for worrying about him.

It has taken years for me to come to terms with our situation and I am still not fully there. Four years on from his diagnosis, I appreciate and love Bobby for all that he is. The autism is there; Bobby has autism. I can say those words now.

Did you research about how to help your child? What did you do? Which organisations/professionals did you reach out to?

I was a woman on a mission. I spent countless hours researching, staying up most nights until 2.00 am searching for something—anything—that would help Bobby. The first thing I did was buy *The Complete Autism Handbook: The Essential Resource Guide for Autism Spectrum Disorder in Australia and New Zealand* by Benison O'Reilly and Kathryn Wicks. It was a fabulous resource with so much useful information about different therapies, as well as stories from other parents. After reading them, I did not feel so alone. I had been feeling guilty for experiencing so much grief and loss and many people around me did not understand, but now I knew other parents who felt the same way as me. Finding this resource and being able to hear from other families helped me so much. I read many other books, which I have listed at the end of my story, starting with Julie Buckley's eye-opening book *Healing Our Autistic Children*, which describes autism as a medical condition (I believe this to be true).

I joined a "MyTime" group that is offered in Sydney. I loved this group. A social worker attends, and it is structured so parents can have a coffee and chat, while the children are supervised and can play. The social worker—the mother of a child with autism and a wealth of information—told me that autism is big business and there are people out there that will take advantage of this. The best advice she gave me was to use a "speed dating" approach with therapists, to see if they are the right ones for your child. These words stuck with me as I went in search for therapists to form our team.

As part of my search for good therapists, I first had paid "parent only" appointments with a psychologist. I quickly realised I had wasted my money as they were not going to be the right fit for us. Next, I did sessions with a speech pathologist specialising in "Relationship Development Intervention"[1], where the parent is trained to be the primary therapist and helps develop relationships and social interactions. A big part of it was an online membership through America where you read a lot of information to begin with. I was too exhausted for this to work; I needed someone to do the therapy for me. I then investigated Applied Behaviour Analysis (ABA)[2] and called a couple of centres that offered this program, but the long hours (up to 30 hours a week) and huge cost of around $50,000–$80,000 (as well as paying for monthly assessments) ruled this out. I was feeling overwhelmed at spending

---

[1] https://en.wikipedia.org/wiki/Relationship_Development_Intervention accessed July 2020

[2] https://raisingchildren.net.au/autism/therapies-guide/aba accessed July 2020

HOW DO I DO THIS?

money and not getting the right outcomes when I stumbled onto the Early Start Denver Model[3] (a version of ABA) and was able to get Bobby into a 10-week program. At the completion of this, I remember breaking down and crying the happiest of tears as I watched my son use eye contact, say hello and goodbye, and wave—all things he had been unable to do before. After we finished the 10-week program, I was still looking for something to continue helping my son, but everything cost a fortune—for example, I was quoted $1,000 for a behavioural therapist just to do an assessment.

Soon after this, I was lucky enough to come across the Plumtree and Lifestart organisations and I was appointed two amazing "key workers" to help me access services. The lady from Plumtree found me our occupational therapist, who is still our therapist four years on, and she also helped me find a pre-school for Bobby where he was well supported for two years. The lady from Lifestart helped me set short and long-term goals. I also started getting smarter and feeling less like a "deer in the headlights" and more in control; I started advocating for Bobby and I began treating these therapists as if they were in a job interview with me. They had to show me *why* I would want to work with them. They had to listen to me talk about who Bobby was and then allow me to question them about how they believed they could best support him. I insisted on speaking to them (for free) prior to committing to the "parent only session" —and I refused to pay for another assessment if I already had one.

Now, with the National Disability Insurance Scheme, the child's goals are what all therapists should be working towards, but it is still important to make sure they are accountable.

The key worker from Plumtree gave me this smart piece of advice:

---

[3] https://www.esdm.co accessed July 2020

"Every time you walk away from any therapy session you should know the following:

1. What are we working on SPECIFICALLY?

2. What does that skill help my child to do? Why is it important for him?

3. What can I do until the next appointment? When I go home what specific targets and activities can I follow through with?

Raise this at the start of the session or email ahead of time to give the therapist time to prepare.

Ask what "short term" goals are you working on. You need to understand and agree with the therapist that the goals are relevant to your child and that you know what you are going to work on during the week.

Remember, you're not being demanding—it is part of a therapist's job to meet these requirements."

What therapies did/do you use? What routines do you find helpful for your child?

Fast forward to our present day and I have a great team around us. Our speech pathologist has been a godsend; she is trained in ABA and her vast knowledge and ability to keep things very play based, and fun, are integrated with our goals to get the right outcomes for Bobby. Our occupational therapist has also been wonderful, helping me navigate my way through tough times and always knowledgeable in how to best approach the goals and outcomes for Bobby. After going through four

HOW DO I DO THIS?

psychologists for various reasons, we finally have one who is also a great part of our team and has helped Bobby with his anxiety, daily struggles, and challenges.

We do a couple of social skills programs that have been invaluable to help Bobby interact with other children, in a safe and supportive way to help him navigate the many layers of communication, play and social skills. Bobby has done the PALS Social Skills Program[4]. I have also investigated the SuperFlex Program [5] and Secret Agent Society[6], and completed the *More than Words*[7] course and Genevieve Jereb's online course *The Traffic Jam in My Brain*[8]. Aspect also run Early Days Workshops which are very helpful and Positive Partnerships run free workshops too.

Bobby thrives on routine and is a visual learner, so pictures or calendars help him understand things much better. They work well and we used them a lot early on but not so much now. Much can get lost in too many spoken words or instructions. My son has a lot of obsessive behaviours where he wants to do the same things repeatedly—for example, many years ago he would happily spend hours lining cars up. While it was his fixed interest, helping him to regulate and stay calm, breaking this took a lot of effort. I found that using "first and then" schedules, timers and limiting the time he could do these things, and redirecting him to other activities, all helped.

---

[4] https://www.learninglinks.org.au/services/children-youth/psychology-programs/social-skills/

[5] https://www.socialmind.com.au/product/superflex-a-superhero-social-thinking-curriculum-package/

[6] https://www.sst-institute.net/

[7] https://raisingchildren.net.au/autism/therapies-guide/more-than-words-

[8] https://shop.sensorytools.net/tjb/index.html all accessed July 2020

Bobby also needs things to be a certain way and as a result he tries to control things. He needed a lot of support with this—for example, he would want a story repeatedly told a certain way and if I deviated from his storyline, he would become very distressed. I had to limit the stories and help him to see that nothing bad would happen if the story changed a bit.

One of the biggest things I have had to learn is to challenge my son. For a long time, I let him avoid things that were difficult for him, but through intervention and helping him to become desensitised to many of the things that he could not cope with, he is now able to function reasonably well. I encourage a lot of bravery.

How has having a child with special needs affected your family? Your marriage?

Having a child with additional needs has deeply affected my family and me. Early on, I struggled a lot, as did my parents. I once read that for grandparents it can be double the grief and I believe this to be accurate. My parents watched me struggle with the diagnosis, as well as having their own fears for their only grandson's future. At first, they were the only people who knew about Bobby's diagnosis. I felt it was nobody else's business and I never wanted anyone to ever look at my son differently. My parents did their best to support me and are the only people who have consistently been there for me. My mother is my best friend and my relationship with her is much stronger now, even through many arguments and sometimes disapproval of how I handled things. As much as they knew I was working hard for Bobby, they often felt he needed more help and getting this help landed squarely on my shoulders. I was incredibly sensitive, sometimes taking their comments with offence and it all seemed to add to my hurt. I knew they were on my team but there were many times that I did not handle things well,

HOW DO I DO THIS?

because I was so crippled by my own grief. Bobby was sucked into a big black hole of autism and I was sucked into a big black hole of grief.

Eventually I did tell my brother and was shocked that he and his partner had suspected for some time that something was amiss with Bobby—yet had said nothing. I was at a loss to understand their reasoning and all I could think of was the valuable time I had wasted to get help for my son. At first my brother was interested to understand the autism and read the sensory processing information I sent him. He wanted to communicate better with Bobby but, like most people, he and his partner found it hard to know how to engage or interact with Bobby and their attempts were often met with silence.

I went on to tell one of Bobby's godmothers, who is a dear friend and works in disability; she understands our situation. Many times, I called her in tears. To this day, she is one of only a few friends that empathises with me. She told me about the poem "*Welcome to Holland*"[9], which seemed to symbolise my life. I took a copy of it for Bobby's other godmother to read, but she did not understand. I sat with Bobby on my lap and told her that he had autism. He looked at me and started hitting me and I realised he could hear and understand everything I was saying about him. It was horrible and I vowed never again to speak like this in front of him. His godmother has been one of the only friends who stood by us, even when Bobby was at one stage having behaviours towards her children. It was a dreadful time as he had little language and so used behaviours to communicate. She was understanding of this, but she did not understand my grief and told me she could not see what the big deal was.

One of my cousins has a son with autism, and when I told her Bobby had been diagnosed with it, her response was "It's not that bad. At least

---

[9] https://emmaplusthree.com/autism/welcome-holland-autism-poem/

he doesn't have cancer". But to me it *was* that bad because at least with cancer there was a set treatment plan. There was help, there was support, there was hope for a cure—you could even get casseroles brought to home by well-meaning family and friends. With autism, there was none of that.

I became an overly anxious person, never feeling safe, always worried and fearing what might happen. Those around me could see this, and they could feel my grief oozing out of me. Like Julie Buckley says in her book about her own feelings over her child's autism, "My grief was palpable". I was no longer the confident, funny, and full of life woman I had been and there was little understanding by my friends and family about my anxiety. Others did not really want to be around me. I told a friend I had known since I was 12 about Bobby's autism, but she did not understand, and I was shattered when I never heard from her again. It was another friendship lost, and another person who seemed to downplay the enormity of how I felt about my son's autism. No-one really seemed to understand my utter devastation.

Relationships in general have been really impacted by my son's autism. People have said things to me that were hurtful and offensive, but I have tried to understand that they often did not know what to say and their words were meant with good intentions and not to hurt. I have needed to be careful who I speak to and I will rarely show the real me. If someone asks how we are, I tell them everything is great. It is an easy answer and it is mostly what people want to hear.

I have not managed to form any friendships with other mothers at the mainstream school Bobby attends, mainly because our lives seem so totally different and I find it incredibly difficult to relate to them. Their problems seem so trivial. I would hear them complain about their child and find it hard to understand why they were just not happy that their child was typically developing and healthy—without the struggles and

HOW DO I DO THIS?

fight that my son had. It was a very bitter pill for me to swallow at times. What they took for granted made me so resentful and angry that I wanted to scream at times!

Every small thing that Bobby fought to learn and achieved was a celebration for me. While other kids were out kicking the ball around, playing sports and having fun, I was trying to teach my son basic things that did not come easily for him. All I could think was "What I wouldn't give for my son to be able to do that" —to not have to spend time in therapy teaching him all the foundation skills, pretend play skills, how to talk to other children and how to catch and throw balls so he could play sport.

Within the autism spectrum, I have found a great divide, with two distinct categories—verbal and non-verbal children. Because Bobby had a large vocabulary, to the autism world he was fine, and his issues were seen to be not as serious as those others faced. Yes, my son could talk but he was unable to converse in a back and forth conversation—and there is a big difference between these two things. Getting other Mums to understand this was difficult; some even told me they did not think Bobby had autism and that I should just be grateful he could talk. This was intensely hurtful, and I felt as though I had to prove my son had autism, just because he had language.

In many ways, I think it is harder for a verbal child, as the mainstream belief is that they do not need additional support, even though their needs are quite high compared to typically developing children. Bobby had quirky behaviours that mainstream children found odd; he would fixate on an interest, making it harder for him to engage in anything else. We also did not fit into the non-verbal world. Many mothers felt the same jealousy towards me that I felt towards typically developing children's parents. Bobby and I did not seem to fit in anywhere, which left us feeling very isolated. Many days, I wondered what life would have looked like without autism.

I have also found that, in the autism world, there are those who believe that autism is part of neurodiversity, that it is genetic and cannot be changed. Then there are those who believe it is a medical condition, a metabolic or gut disorder triggered by something in the environment—and symptoms can improve with dietary and medical interventions. I sat in the latter category of autism, seeing with my own eyes my son's improvement with a change to a diet free of sugar and processed foods. I faced ridicule from some family and friends for my beliefs, and, to save the confrontational discussions, I have learned to keep these to myself.

Through my journey of autism, some relationships have suffered and were lost, and some new ones have begun. About two years after Bobby's diagnosis, I found the world of other Mums who had children with autism. I felt like I had won the lottery because these mothers understood. I am so grateful for these beautiful women who have listened and been an amazing sounding board and who I have been able to also help and support. When Bobby was five, I met a mother who was to become one of my best friends. I talk to her most days and am so blessed by her friendship. She is someone that I can safely cry to; scream, laugh and joke with; and who "gets" it. I think everyone needs just one person who understands, who shows compassion and empathy without judgment. I would not swap those friendships for the world. Without autism, I never would have met and come to know these wonderful people.

HOW DO I DO THIS?

How do you take care of yourself? What self-care strategies do you use and how have you been able to implement them?

For the longest time, I was consumed with autism. It ruled my life, and, in many ways, it still does. There was no time for me, just the world of autism and trying to find ways to give my son a better life. I said once to a psychologist that I will be fine if Bobby is fine. The psychologist pointed out that it may be a long time before Bobby would be okay and so I needed to start looking after myself. I found this hard to do. It felt wrong to have "me" time, like I was being self-indulgent when my son needed so much help.

My biggest self-care is finding ways to be a little kinder to myself, recognising that I do a lot to help Bobby and that I am not a failure because I "should" be doing more. As the saying goes, autism is not a sprint but a marathon and so I have had to learn to slow down and pace myself and look after both my son and me. To help me cope, I have had to adapt some strategies, some of which I have learned through my son's therapy sessions—taking deep breaths, counting to 10 and regulating my own emotions. Mindfulness courses have helped, where I learned to welcome in the grief, the sadness and anger that often knocked on my door. I read *Buddhism for Mothers* by Sarah Napthali, *The Push for a Child Philosophy* by Dr Maxine Therese, and some other books for my own growth by Iyanla Vanzant, to try to help me grow into a better, more resilient person through my own emotional rollercoaster ride.

I have had to learn to switch my brain off; to stop what I call the freight train running through my head. Instead of comparing Bobby with other children and feeling grief, I accept and love my son for all that he is, to try to find some peace in my heart. I have stopped reading until 2.00 am in the morning and I now tend to spend my nights watching Netflix, escaping the world of autism through a television series that allows me an hour or so of rest from my own thoughts. Occasionally, I indulge in a massage to help with my back complaints. I make sure I have a shower every day and on the days I need it most, I stay in a little longer and let the water run through my hair, hoping to wash away all the hurt and pain that I carry in me. What has helped me the most is going for walks, and, if I can, getting down to the beach to appreciate the blue of the water and the wind in my face. I also recently took up learning the piano, which is something that I enjoy doing and which gives me a small sense of my own achievement.

Finding an amazing counsellor—herself a mother of a child with autism—has been another blessing and has helped me more than anyone. She has been my rock, and, with her listening ear and steadfast guidance, has helped me to advocate throughout Bobby's schooling. I understand myself better and, although I am still a work in progress operating in survival mode a lot of the time, I hope one day I can move beyond this and begin to thrive.

How important/necessary is your family support or the support of your friends/networks? Do you feel as though you have enough support?

Having good support is vital but I do not feel as though I have enough. When I was young, I was raised by a village, but this is no longer. Having some support and some type of village around is crucial. I could not have done this on my own. I have been so fortunate to have my parents who try their best to help us and support us—for example, my Mum helps me by cooking food for Bobby and my Dad helps by taking him for walks to give me a break. Understanding friends I can talk to and rely on to get me through some very tough days, as well as my wonderful counsellor, have all been an incredible support.

HOW DO I DO THIS?

Outside of that, some groups on Facebook have been helpful and I have met some nice friends through there, as well as some Mums in the waiting room at therapy sessions. Strangers are also some of the nicest people you can meet. They listen, they do not judge, they are sympathetic and at the end of talking, you can walk away and never have to see them again. Autism Community Network (ACN) also hold a lot of different activities for kids and parent support groups.

What do you hope/think the future holds for your child? Their living arrangements? A job? Marriage and children of their own?

I try not to think about the future too much as it creates a lot of fear for me. Those first fears I had of my son's future right after his diagnosis are something that come back to taunt me at times. At the same time, I do believe and hope that Bobby will have a future that can be a happy one, and I can still have all those hopes and dreams for him.

I try to take one day at a time and work towards Bobby gaining the skills to live independently, make friends, cope at school and be more resilient. My hope for my son is that he grows to be whoever he is meant to be, living out whatever his dreams are. I can only hope that he is happy and healthy, and lives a long life, where he is loved, understood, and accepted. I want him to be able to engage with his peers and have friendships. Of course, as he gets older, I hope that he will find a partner or someone who is a companion.

I believe that Bobby will be successful because he is an amazing little boy who has faced such adversity and still comes out the other end so happy. If this journey has taught me anything, it is to believe in how strong and courageous he is.

AGE GROUP 7-12

What are/have been the joys of raising your child?

Having Bobby has been the most precious gift that I could have ever been given and I have been absolutely blessed to have him as my son. He is a delight to raise and the joy of raising him is that he is just Bobby. Regardless of a label or having the traits of a label, my son is still the most beautiful, kind, gentle and precious little boy and I sometimes wonder how I could be so fortunate as to be given a child with such a beautiful nature.

Bobby has always been so happy, with a good sense of humour and always sees the funny side to things. He wakes up every day with a smile on his face and happiness in his voice and heart. His laughter is something that brings so much joy to me, to his grandparents and to the people around him. His first smile is something I will always remember, and the smiles he brings to our lives every single day are something I treasure.

I admire Bobby's strength and resilience. He tackles anything put in front of him and does so with such persistence and character. I admire his fight, watching him overcome such big fears and be able to do things he never dreamed of doing. I admire that he never gives up!

Hearing him call me "Mum Mum" are words that I cherish. Being able to hold his tiny hand in mine has brought so much joy. Every night, I have loved watching him fall asleep and every day, I have loved watching him grow into a more confident little boy.

What are/have been the hardest challenges raising your child?

The hardest challenges in raising my child have been my own lack of understanding of his diagnosis and his needs, and the way that this impacts him. I did not fully understand the extent of his diagnosis, and of the total unpredictability of autism, sensory processing, and anxiety. I worked this out myself through some research, but mostly by living with autism. There is no manual on how your child will behave or react in certain situations. Having a 40-minute meltdown because a biscuit broke in half were incredibly challenging and heartbreaking times to live through. Because the meltdowns could be so intense and I did not know how to react, there were times I could not comfort or console my son. These times were incredibly hard for Bobby, who was in sheer pain, as though he was tormented over things that would not bother most of us. I felt totally helpless, not knowing how to help him.

The rigid traits of autism were also difficult to deal with and there were days it drove me crazy. Trying to ignore the constant repetition was often a huge struggle. I also found it incredibly hard not being able to have typical interactions of play and conversations with Bobby. The mother/child relationship was disrupted because I was unable to interact the same way I would with a typically developing child. My attempts to play, engage and have conversations with my son were often met with silence, which left me feeling so lost in trying to develop a normal relationship with him.

Despite there being more awareness, the lack of understanding about autism by family, friends and people in general has been difficult. Instead of being recognised as a direct part of his diagnosis, Bobby's behaviours were judged as poor, rather than his only way to communicate or express how he was feeling as he tried desperately to cope in an overwhelming world. I would show my son empathy or compassion and try to understand what he was going through but I was often criticised for this approach, as though my parenting was flawed. I was lectured on setting boundaries and not letting Bobby "get away with things".

AGE GROUP 7-12

If we had more understanding people around us, life would have been easier for both my son and me. The judgment and isolation are like being in a constant battle with the world—fighting to be "believed" and advocating for my son's needs to be understood and met is exhausting and very hurtful. School has been especially difficult and traumatising for both Bobby and me. Since he started school two years ago, it has been a never-ending battle. Due to their lack of understanding or ability to implement even basic accommodations of support, there have been constant meetings with teachers, Principals, and the Department of Education.

What has your child taught you?

Bobby is my greatest teacher; he has taught me so much. Because of who he is, I feel I have grown and evolved in many ways to become a stronger and better person and parent. I recognise that the things he may do are because of his autism and not because he is doing them on purpose. My son has taught me to re-evaluate my responses to situations and I now have better ways of dealing with the unpredictability of autism. I have learned what advocating for your child really means.

I am no longer judging of others and I now have a different level of empathy and compassion. I have learned patience and understanding of so many different things. Bobby has helped me to see that everyone is going through something, and we should always choose kindness and understanding first.

How do you view your child's special needs?

Bobby's special needs have been difficult for me. I do acknowledge that the autism is a part of who he is and, in many ways, makes him even more special and beautiful. I embrace my child, but I have found it intensely difficult to embrace autism. I love my son with every piece there is of me, but it is hard some days to love autism. At times, the lines seemed to blur because there were many days that I looked at my son and all I saw was autism. I have never wanted Bobby's autism to define him.

Bobby was not born with autism, and I believe it was caused by environmental factors. I believe my son has an underlying medical condition and, like any medical condition, I would like treatment and a cure.

What would you say to other parents of special needs children just beginning their journey? What advice/suggestions would you have for them?

It can be incredibly overwhelming in the beginning, like being in the densest jungle with no map. You must take things slowly, one day at a time. It is a long road, so you do have to pace yourself.

Try to get a good team of therapists around you, but buyer beware! Be aware that autism is big business, and everyone is selling something. Cherry pick what is right for your child and you. Do not get sucked into buying things or doing therapies that you do not need. Investigate biomedical interventions and changes in diet for your child.

Be kind to yourself. Allow yourself to grieve if you need to. Grief is cyclical and the smallest things can set it off. Do not get lost in the disability.

Remember also to smile, let the sun shine on your face and never forget who you are.

AGE GROUP 7-12

If you could think of one word to describe being a parent of a child with special needs what would it be?

Hard.

Any final thoughts?

Do your own research. Never apologise for advocating for your child or for their behaviour; every behaviour is a communication. Set short-and long-term goals to help you work your way through all the different types of therapy. Get a village around you. Laugh even on the days you cry. Believe in yourself and believe in your child.

Please list any organisations and resources that you have found helpful.

<u>Organisations</u>

- Aspect Early Days Workshops – www.autismspectrum.org.au/how-can-we-help/attend-a-workshop/early-days-workshops

- Positive Partnerships – www.positivepartnerships.com.au

- Plumtree www.plumtree.org.au

- Lifestart Early Childhood Intervention Supports – www.lifestart.org.au

- Koorana Child and Family Services – www.koorana.org.au

HOW DO I DO THIS?

- Autism Community Network – www.autismcommunity.org.au
- Learning Links – www.learninglinks.org.au

Books

"The Australian Autism Handbook" – Benison O'Reilly and Kathryn Wicks

"Ten Things Every Child with Autism Wishes you Knew" – Ellen Notbohm

"The Verbal Behaviour Approach: How to Teach Children with Autism and Related Disorders" – Dr Mary Lynch Barbera

"The Out of Sync Child" – Carol Stock Kranowitz

"No More Meltdowns" – Jed Baker

"Managing Anxiety in People with Autism" – Anne M. Chalfant

"More Than Words" – Fern Sussman

"An Early Start for your child with Autism" – Rogers, Dawson and Vismara

"Healing Our Autistic Children – A Medical Plan for Restoring Your Child's Health" – Julie A. Buckley

"Can we manage Autism, Yes we Can" – Jan Brenton

"Children's Health" – Dr Leila Masson

"The Myth of Autism" – Dr. Michael J Goldberg

"Nutrient Power" – Dr. William J. Walsh

"How to End the Autism Epidemic" – J.B. Handley

"Gut and Psychology Syndrome" – Dr. Natasha Campbell-McBride

AGE GROUP 7-12

"Autism and Attention Deficit Disorders – Understanding and Managing Diet Therapy for Your Child" – Judith Salmon and Leanne Pearce

"The Autism Vaccine – The Story of Modern Medicine's Greatest Tragedy" – Forrest Maready

"Breaking the Vicious Cycle" – Elaine Gottschall

"FOOD What the Heck Should I Eat" – Mark Hyman

"High Thrive Me, A 5-step guide to helping kids with autism live happier, healthier lives" – Kris Barrett

"No Cows Today, A Mother's Story. A Son's Recovery" – Kris Barrett

"Living with Max" – Chloe Maxwell

"Buddhism for Mothers" – Sarah Napthali

"The Push for a Child Philosophy" – Dr. Maxine Therese

Practitioners:

- Kris Barrett – www.krisbarrett.com.au
- Jillaine Williams – Pantry Practitioner – www.pantrypractitioner.com.au
- Lily Holland – www.lilyholland.com
- Sue Larkey – www.suelarkey.com.au

DIANA, SCOTT, RACHEL, DAVID, SADIE AND BECCA (USA)

Introduction:

My name is Diana Kerkis and my family is Dad (Scott), Rachel (17), David (14), and our twin girls Becca and Sadie, who are 9 and turning 10 on October 13. We live in Bentonville, Arkansas, in the USA.

Becca is considered severely autistic and she makes a lot of little noises and hums, but there are no words at all. She is also developmentally delayed—we are unsure as to what overall "age" she is because each developmental facet is different.

Was it always apparent to you that your child had special needs? If not, when did you notice that something was "different" about your child?

I had a problem-free pregnancy with the twins. Becca and Sadie were born prematurely, but they were the size of full-term babies—Becca was 6 lbs and Sadie was the slightly bigger (at 7 lbs) and older (by one minute) twin. The babies were healthy and at first it was not apparent that there were any problems. Becca was always happy, but by the time she was about six months of age there began to be some concerns. For example, Becca would just sit and stare out the window and would not attempt to get around or crawl. One time I had accidentally stepped on her little finger and she did not even cry or make a sound; I know it would have really hurt and I thought that was odd. Sadie was thriving but Becca was not, so we thought we would have to take her in to get her evaluated.

If you have received a formal diagnosis for your child's special needs, when did this happen? Do you remember what feelings you experienced at the time and was the diagnosis a hard thing to come to terms with? Have you come to terms with it?

Becca was 18 months old when she was diagnosed, and my first feeling was proactive— "What can we do to help here?" I just wanted to make sure she would get the help she needed. I never mourned for the child she could have been. I know Scott felt that way also.

HOW DO I DO THIS?

I have come to terms with her diagnosis. Becca is Becca and we accept her for who she is. She is such a sweet little girl and happy and pretty relaxed 85% of the time. It is not hard and nor is it easy, but we love Becca, and we would do anything for her.

Did you research about how to help your child? What did you do? Which organisations/professionals did you reach out to?

In the USA when you first plug in to get help, the first thing that comes up is "Autism Speaks". At first, I thought they were great, but a little later I realised that some of the things they believe in are not so great.

I am thankful for Facebook because that's where I met a lot of my contacts: for example, "World of Autism: Making It An Ausome Positive One!", where I have met a lot of adult autistic people who have helped with questions I have had and given me information. There is also a group called "Autism Involves Me (AIM)" and they have a great local chapter where the families meet up and we also do monthly meetups with the Moms.

Becca's paediatrician was extremely helpful because he is a father and grandfather to a lot of special needs kids. Becca started Applied Behaviour Analysis (ABA) when she was about three years of age and it has really helped us—I think because she is so severe and has so many behaviours that we have tried to correct. It has also helped ease the load on me because there are so many times where it is just me and her. Becca paces a lot and she will come by me and tap me or pull me to look at her in the eyes to let me know she is there.

It is difficult for me to do the things I need to do—cooking, loading the dishwasher and so on—so I can do those things when the ABA therapist is here. We have had some great therapists as well as some bad ones. School is out right now because of the COVID19 pandemic lockdown, so the therapists come to us Monday to Friday from 12.30 until 6 pm.

What therapies did/do you use? What routines do you find helpful for your child?

In the beginning, we did all the therapies at once—speech, occupational therapy, and physiotherapy—and each of them helped in different aspects. For example, Becca's fine motor skills are still not developed. For speech, we concentrated more on the eating aspect rather than on the actual talking but this is something I want to do a little later.

Our family is just such a crazy family and I am not the most organised person in the world, but we always have a specific time for meals, bath, and bedtime.

How has having a child with special needs affected your family? Your marriage? Your other children?

I think it has been hardest on Sadie in that she says no-one ever talks about me, only Becca. Sadie is very funny and creative and is her own child. She helps so much with Becca and is very mature for her age; she is like an old soul, and she knows how to calm Becca down and make her laugh and be happy.

The older kids were five and eight when the twins were born, and I think they had enough attention up to that point to be okay with Becca needing so much more attention.

It was hard on our marriage. Scott and I very rarely had time to ourselves, or got to go out. There was only one person who we trusted to watch all the kids at the same time and she eventually got married and had her own family.

Sadly, Scott and I have now separated and are going through a divorce.

How do you take care of yourself? What self-care strategies do you use and how have you been able to implement them?

I have my own Younique home-based business, and this has certainly helped a lot. With special needs kids, you stay home so much and so dealing with Younique and being on Facebook is the only way I socialise. I deal with all my business on there, I have all my Younique sisters as well as other friends. Younique has given me the avenue to be able to help women feel beautiful and to help themselves to accept themselves as they are.

I work out at least six days a week which really helps with the stress; even if it is a quick 35-or-40-minute workout a day, I do that. That is all the time I have.

Do you have a faith? If so, how has this helped you cope with life with your child?

I was raised Catholic and I went to Catholic school, so that has given me a good basis for my faith and to know what is right and wrong. I may not always do the right thing, but if I do the wrong thing, I know it. Scott is Jewish, so we tried to introduce both faiths.

Sadie and I just started to go back to church before the pandemic hit. I have always been spiritual and believed in God and in the power of prayer a whole lot.

I believe God put us on this earth for a certain reason and that is why we were given Becca and our family. I feel Becca is a definite blessing.

How important/necessary is your family support or the support of your friends/networks? Do you feel as though you have enough support?

I was extremely close to my family—my Mom and three brothers (my Dad passed away)—until, unfortunately, we had to move. I talk to my Mom on the phone several times a day and I have become close to my cousin in Colorado since the divorce thing has happened. Being on the phone that way has really helped.

I would say Facebook is my way to socialise and gain support and that is where most of my friends are. I have met so many great people; I have so many Australian and Canadian friends who for me are just as close as people I grew up with.

I think I get enough support. I am an only girl with three brothers and so I have always been independent; otherwise, I probably would have caved a long time ago and not been able to handle all this. I have always been self-reliant and used to picking myself back up and motivating myself to just keep going.

What do you hope/think the future holds for your child? Their living arrangements? A job? Marriage and children of their own?

Now that Becca is going on 10 years of age, I can see her maturing and I worry about her and what is going to happen. I feel truly fortunate she has Sadie but then again, I do not want Sadie to feel she is 100% in charge of her sister—even though she has said it is going to be her and Becca together. But I think we need to wait and see.

The kids were telling me at the schools they see the special needs kids as the ones who help to clean up the cafeteria and so on. I believe that Becca could do so much more than menial labour like that; I want better for her. I am thinking more and more of taking her out of regular school and putting her into the ABA Clinic, which a lot of the special needs' kids use as their school.

The future is wide open for Becca and I am hoping to keep researching and finding out new things for her to learn; she still has a lot of growing to do. There are hopes that she will get married and have a family but at this point I am not sure about this.

What are/have been the joys of raising your child?

I think just being able to see just how happy Becca can be. She has this pure joy when she does things—for example, to see her outside jumping on the trampoline, just being happy. That has been the greatest thing.

I love my other kids, but you do not realise the love you have for your children until you have raised a special needs kid. I would do anything for all my children but with Becca, I really *know* that I love her.

What are/have been the hardest challenges raising your child?

The main challenge is the physical side of taking care of Becca. I still need to bathe and change her. She is being potty trained but she is not there yet and so I have to change her diapers. She is different with her therapists but when I am changing her, she will push me and kick me and then I'm rolling backwards. This is not intentional, but Becca does not know her own strength. She is just so strong! And that is hard for me. Also, her motor skills are not there, and it is difficult for her to wipe herself and know she is clean. Becca can feed herself, but I still need to make sure the food is in front of her and she is eating it. It is also up to me to make sure she gets her meds every day.

Becca still drinks bottles throughout the night. I do not see any way of stopping this because where once she used to go back to sleep, now she will sit up and want that bottle. Becca does go through phases of not drinking a lot and I think the bottle is more of a comfort thing than anything else. My sleep is constantly disturbed to give Becca the bottle because she whimpers, and I will tend to her. It is a little better on weekends because then Scott has the kids but during the week, I do not get to sleep a whole lot.

Because Becca is getting older now, I have started thinking about what it will be like once she hits puberty. My Mom, who is 80, talks about giving Becca something so she is not able to have babies, but this is not a choice that I am willing to take away from her.

I have also heard that there is medication that can slow down the puberty process and I might try that with Becca, as she is not mentally at the level to handle this just yet.

What has your child taught you?

Becca has taught me resilience, patience that I never knew I had; as well as the gumption to keep going and to take care of yourself because you want to be around as long as you can for your child. Because she is non-verbal and can't speak for herself, Becca has taught me how to advocate for her. There have been so many times—for example, at her school— that I have had to be very blunt and upfront about certain things not being taken care of. I have had to learn to stand up for myself and for Becca, and this has also made me more aware for my other kids.

How do you view your child's special needs?

So many people are like, "I hate the autism and I love the child" but for me autism is the child and I do not separate the two. Autism is part of who Becca is and it makes her who she is.

What would you say to other parents of special needs children just beginning their journey? What advice/suggestions would you have for them?

I would say to just love and support your child. They are your baby and you are their voice and their advocate; you are the one who will protect, nurture, and support them.

So many parents think "What about me?" and I say, "You decided to have this child and you gotta support them."

That is ultimately the final say: you are their everything.

If you could think of one word to describe being a parent of a child with special needs what would it be?

Strength.

AGE GROUP 7-12

Any final thoughts?

Just that I would not know life any different. We have been dealt this card and we are playing it. This is life! This is how it is. We have been blessed with Becca and that is it. We keep going.

Please list any organisations in your country that you have found helpful.

- Autism Involves Me (AIM) at https://aimnwa.org. Their mission is to enhance the lives of people with autism by connecting the NW Arkansas community through greater awareness and resources.

- First Connections – Arkansas Network of Home and Community-based Early Intervention at https://dhs.arkansas.gov/dds/firstconnectionsweb which provides support and services for families and their children, birth to age three, who have special needs. They are a state-wide, comprehensive early intervention network of qualified, dedicated professionals to work directly with your family to custom design a plan with you to meet your child's and your family's needs. They helped a lot; Becca was one of the first kids on their waiver and that helped me navigate things.

- BlueSprig Autism, providing ABA Therapy, https://bluesprigautism.com.

- The International Facebook group:
  World of Autism: Making it an Ausome Positive One!
  https://www.facebook.com/groups/585825561505059/?ref=share

HOW DO I DO THIS?

- To contact Diana about her online business Younique you can connect with Diana on Facebook: Diana Moore-Kerkis.

- Becca and Sadie's story "Sadie for Becca…and Becca for Sadie" was featured in **Peekaboo: Northwest Arkansas' Family Magazine** in October 2018, page 40. You can find this issue of the magazine at: www.peekaboonwa.com. Go to Magazine and all past issues will be shown.

MARTA, TAN AND DIEGO (UNITED KINGDOM)

Introduction:

My name is Marta. I am married to Tan and the Mom of a nonverbal autistic boy, Diego, who is nine years old. We live in Edinburgh.

Was it always apparent to you that your child had special needs? If not, when did you notice that something was "different" about your child?

Despite Diego being extremely premature (born at 26 weeks) and with a low birth weight (510 grams), he did not seem to have any disability until he was 18 months old. Even though his speech was delayed, the doctors believed this was caused by his prematurity. At that time, I noticed that Diego was not actually communicating, as he would not make any kind of signs like pointing or nodding.

If you have received a formal diagnosis for your child's special needs, when did this happen? Do you remember what feelings you experienced at the time and was the diagnosis a hard thing to come to terms with? Have you come to terms with it?

Diego was formally diagnosed with autism when he was nearly three years old. Knowing what the outcome of this would most likely be, I was in shock and I experienced a whole range of emotions. It was hard. My whole world sank. I had an idea of what the autism diagnosis meant, and I feared for my child. Would he ever be able to be independent? I also felt ashamed, as though I had done something wrong and was somehow responsible for Diego's autism.

I felt extremely angry, scared, and completely lost. Six years later, I still struggle but I have come to terms with the diagnosis.

Did you research about how to help your child? What did you do? Which organisations/professionals did you reach out to?

The first time I raised the concern (when Diego was 18 months old), the professionals told me to research autism, which I did. It really demoralised me though. The first website I accessed back then (more than seven years ago) was Autism Speaks, and their fatalistic take on autism did not help me at all.

AGE GROUP 7-12

I then found the National Autistic Society (NAS) website where I found a lot of helpful information about therapies, schools and so on. The sad part of this is that I realised the best schools for autistic children were exorbitantly expensive, and so I despaired. It seems that the only way of getting the right support for your child in the United Kingdom is if you are a millionaire.

What therapies did/do you use? What routines do you find helpful for your child?

We tried EVERYTHING with my child, including PECs and Makaton (sign language). However, without routinely consistent help from professionals it was so difficult—almost impossible—but still we have tried. It is really exasperating to think you may have tried this speech language therapy with your child for years, only to find out that you are doing it incorrectly simply because you do not have access to the right professionals who can tell you what you are doing wrong. You feel you let your child down (again) because you did not study to become a speech or occupational therapist.

The most helpful routines for us have been the bedtime routine and other self-care routines. We found this helps Diego's independence skills.

How has having a child with special needs affected your family? Your marriage?

First, it stopped us from having other children. Knowing that the cause for autism has a genetic component, we did not want to risk having another child with the same disability. As a result, my husband and I had a lot of fights, and due to the trauma of the whole situation (prematurity/disability "combo") I sank into a depression and was also formally diagnosed with anxiety. The fact that there was no help or support for my child (or me) made things much worse. I believe I was suffering from PTSD (post-traumatic stress disorder)[10] and I became verbally aggressive towards my husband, which was very unfair to him. I also saw how my moods were affecting me physically—with headaches, feeling physically sick, high blood pressure and so on. I can see why so many couples break up after having a special needs child, because of all the difficulties that are linked, which then becomes this massive issue that is almost impossible to solve.

How do you take care of yourself? What self-care strategies do you use and how have you been able to implement them?

My husband and I are both foreigners from different countries, and so we have no family help whatsoever. Basically, my self-care time is when my child goes to sleep. I can have maybe one or two hours for myself and I can relax and watch a movie or read a book. I realise I must do more, but I just cannot find the extra time and the "energy resources" for this.

Do you have a faith? If so, how has this helped you cope with life with your child?

No. We follow Buddhist philosophy.

---

[10] https://www.mayoclinic.org/diseases-conditions/post-traumatic-stress-disorder/symptoms-causes/syc-20355967 accessed April 2020

AGE GROUP 7-12

How important/necessary is your family support or the support of your friends/networks? Do you feel as though you have enough support?

We think it could be extremely important but, to be honest, we do not have this type of support at all and so we do struggle.

What do you hope/think the future holds for your child? Their living arrangements? A job? Marriage and children of their own?

My child is severely autistic and thinking about his future (in our current society) is one of the things that most depresses me.

What are/have been the joys of raising your child?

I have learned to live in the moment without judgments and to be more patient. I have learned what is most important in life and I value little things so much more.

What are/have been the hardest challenges raising your child?

The ignorance of others (including people within the autism community) has been extremely hard. There is a lack of support, provisions, early intervention help and preparation for the educational system. It is also hard to have to depend on professionals and their scrutiny into our family life. It seems to me that only parents abusing their children get the same type of scrutiny.

HOW DO I DO THIS?

What has your child taught you?

Diego has taught me endurance, resilience, patience, humility, understanding and empathy.

How do you view your child's special needs?

Autism is a disability in my child. It is a difficulty, and the co-morbid conditions around it just makes it harder for Diego to navigate anything in this life.

I believe all children are unique, regardless of whether they have special needs or not. I can still understand how others less negatively affected by a condition may look at this as a gift, but as we are all unique, this may vary depending on the person—and this fact should be respected by everybody.

I, personally, have no other choice but to embrace my child's special needs, as this is a major part of his life and it is not helpful for anybody to live in denial.

I also embrace it, to learn the best ways on how to support my child, but I will never romanticise it or celebrate it.

What would you say to other parents of special needs children just beginning their journey? What advice/ suggestions would you have for them?

Always respect your child and always presume competence (regardless of how severely disabled your child is).

It is okay to make mistakes; we are all human beings.

AGE GROUP 7-12

Listen to your gut and never let anybody dictate to you how you should feel, how you should behave (including me, right now). Seek groups that may understand you. Enjoy your child and your life as a family.

Sadly, as the world is still hostile to our children and families, prepare for battle! Nobody will fight this fight for your child; only you can fight it and be their advocate. Inform yourself, learn the laws and organise to meet with other local parents/carers.

Never give up! You got this!

If you could think of one word to describe being a parent of a child with special needs what would it be?

Fighters!

Please list any organisations in your country that you have found helpful.

United Kingdom:

- Autistica: Working with autistic people and families on research that matters: https://www.autistica.org.uk/

- National Autistic Society: https://www.autism.org.uk/

- Independent Provider of Special Education Advice: https://www.ipsea.org.uk/

HOW DO I DO THIS?

- Parents for our children's futures: https://sendpact.com/

- Parent led information, resources and informed opinion about children and young people 0-25: https://www.specialneedsjungle.com/

FRANCESCA AND NATHAN (AUSTRALIA)

Introduction:

My name is Francesca and I live in Melbourne with my partner Jan and my son Nathan. Nathan is 11 years old, with an intellectual age of four, and he has autism. Since he was in Prep, he has attended the Southern Autistic School in East Bentleigh.

HOW DO I DO THIS?

Was it always apparent to you that your child had special needs? If not, when did you notice that something was "different" about your child?

This has always been apparent to me. When Nathan was four months old, he had a seizure. The hospital was determined that it was a convulsion but afterwards I knew it was a seizure, because Nathan started becoming unresponsive.

If you have received a formal diagnosis for your child's special needs, when did this happen? Do you remember what feelings you experienced at the time and was the diagnosis a hard thing to come to terms with? Have you come to terms with it?

I began noticing delays in Nathan's development, and at six months of age, he was diagnosed with global developmental delay. At 12 months of age, doctors said Nathan might have had cerebral palsy, but no-one was able to determine exactly what was wrong with him.

I ended up seeing four different paediatricians, because my gut feeling was telling me there was more to Nathan's grunting and flapping of his hands, and the frustration that was coming through him. I was getting more and more upset and frustrated at not having a diagnosis and my GP could see this, and so he referred me onto a paediatrician who he knew personally at the Royal Children's Hospital in Melbourne[11]. At the age of four, Nathan was finally diagnosed with autism by this paediatrician. Straight away, as soon as he saw Nathan, he was able to determine that he had something like autism. He told me he saw many children like Nathan.

---

[11] https://www.rch.org.au/home accessed April 2020

I experienced relief because I was able to begin focusing on how I could help and support Nathan to get the therapy he needed to start moving forward.

It was not hard to come to terms with the diagnosis; for me, the hardest part had been running around trying to find out what was wrong. When I did, I felt relief and determination to put things in place for Nathan.

Did you research about how to help your child? What did you do? Which organisations/professionals did you reach out to?

Definitely! I spoke to a lot of therapists, especially speech and occupational therapists. I had a lot of guidance and support from Scope Melbourne (Early Intervention Services) which allocated services for children with global development delay in areas like relationships, nutrition, environment and play time.

I also had a lovely social worker who sat down with me and asked what I was looking for to support Nathan. What I wanted was to expand into the community and to see what was out there to support Nathan.

What therapies did/do you use? What routines do you find helpful for your child?

For the last ten years, I have been using a paediatric psychologist for Nathan for behaviours, as well as occupational and speech therapy, and physiotherapy.

Nathan likes structure so what has been helpful is using visuals for normal daily activities. Nathan is good at time, days, and dates so basically, I follow through with this. If we are doing something different, I usually talk through it with him before it happens.

He uses a visual timetable at school, and we had this at home for a little while, but Nathan wanted to take control, so I had to stop.

I do still use visuals for the toilet as Nathan has poor hand coordination. He is not able to open his hands properly and his fingers are very weak, so he needs help with wiping.

How has having a child with special needs affected your family? Your marriage or relationship?

It has been hard. I come from a European family who did not believe anything was wrong with Nathan and believed I wanted him to have special needs for attention or sympathy. I had to make them understand that this is how Nathan is and this is what you do to follow through. It was quite challenging because there were certain behaviours they should not act on because I knew Nathan would not understand it was play, or being silly, or it was a game. My parents found this hard and they got frustrated easily and they used to yell at him. My Mum wanted me to act differently instead of me being accepting of how Nathan is. They just could not understand how I could be positive about the whole thing and how bright and forward I was.

My brother and sister treated Nathan as though they did not know what to do with him—how to interact with him and talk to him. They made it more awkward than what it was.

As soon as Nathan was diagnosed, his father told me "I want you to fix him" and then walked out on us. I already had a lot of issues with him; he was a gambler from overseas who just wanted to get his residency and had gotten me pregnant just so he could stay in Australia. When we got our pregnancy scan, he said he was glad it was a boy so he could look after me. As soon as he got his residency, he did not want a bar of us. He never gave Nathan much attention.

How do you take care of yourself? What self-care strategies do you use and how have you been able to implement them?

I love my painting and I use it as a way of self-care. I also enjoy taking the time to go for walks, spend time with friends and see my psychologist. Sometimes it is good for your mind to talk to someone, to get that support you need. Work is also my way out and it has always given me the opportunity to switch off at times. And coffee! I love my coffee!

If I know Nathan is settled during the day, doing something for himself, that gives me the opportunity to do something for myself. It is just about knowing when Nathan is in a good space and not needing much of my attention, so I can take the time for me. If I am painting, he sees me calm; so, he calms. I have a little egg chair that I sit in and I can swing in it and it helps me to feel calm.

I also get carers in to look after Nathan, so that gives me the time as well.

Do you have a faith? If so, how has this helped you cope with life with your child?

I definitely have a faith. It is being able to just know, deep down, that I am not on my own. Knowing that, when it gets tough, God is looking after me and Nathan; and that it is all part of a plan. I leave it to God to help me through tough times. I say a little prayer. With my faith, comes believing in myself that I have been given a gift and how to do this. I have faith that we are going to get through this.

How important/necessary is your family support or the support of your friends/networks? Do you feel as though you have enough support?

I think these are definitely important, but at the end of the day I need to be aware that I have to do this on my own; to do this with my child because I am the only one who knows him—and then, having the strength to know that I can do this.

It is great to have friends around, but at times when they are not, I can continue to take those steps forward. Sometimes when I really need the support the most, I don't have it, and so I have to work around this and accept it and know that I can still do this. In the beginning with Nathan, I never had support, so I had to work around how I was going to do this and work through it with ways to know and accept that I am on my own.

I do have Jan, but he is so busy, and the reality is if I did not have Jan, then I am pretty much stuck. When Jan is not here and if anything happens and I am needing to reach out to people, I must figure out who to reach out to. I have been having recent health issues and ever since I have not been well, this has been a big concern. I have felt anxious about what is going to happen with Nathan, so I am working towards fostering and getting a family involved. I do need to put things in place now that this has all happened.

AGE GROUP 7-12

What do you hope/think the future holds for your child? Their living arrangements? A job? Marriage and children of their own?

I want Nathan to feel loved, to feel safe and be healthy.

I certainly want him to live independently and to be able to think for himself; to find a beautiful partner, have kids and live a normal life. I want him to also be aware that life will not be easy, and he will be going through challenges; and to know what to do, so he comes through.

What are/have been the joys of raising your child?

There are so many! It is the little milestones that Nathan achieves that mean so much and are the biggest moments for me; the small steps that for others mean nothing but for me they are such a big step and mean so much. For example, his writing. Nathan made a sign for his bed when he did not want to be in bed anymore. To see what he had written— "No sip (sleep) in bed" was huge and so precious to me. His first words and then every new word were big milestones and brought such joy.

Nathan does get obsessive about Christmas trees, Christmas lights and fireworks and when he starts focusing on something else besides these things—it is the best! He really does shine. He has a lot of empathy and he is extremely sensitive; he cries listening to music. There will be a happy song on, and he will start crying.

He is also so funny. For example, one time he approached a homeless man who had a bottle, and he said to the man "Is that Coke you're drinking?" to which the man replied "Oh no" and Nathan said "That Coke's no good for you; it's gonna make you sick". He has no filter; he will just say things as they are.

HOW DO I DO THIS?

What are/have been the hardest challenges raising your child?

My hardest challenge with Nathan is around not seeing his grandparents. Because they are not supportive, I have had to shut the doors on my family, to protect Nathan and me. He does miss his grandparents and he has a lot of anger, frustration, and resentment towards me because he doesn't see them. I know there is a lot going on with him trying to understand the situation and it breaks my heart.

It is what it is, and I had to make a big choice and it has not been easy. I have always been praying for peace about it.

What has your child taught you?

I have learned so much and Nathan has been my inspiration! He has taught me that sometimes in life you do not get what you want—but by accepting what you have, life becomes a lot easier.

I have so much gratitude because of him.

I have had to fight for what is best for Nathan; it is all about being his eyes, ears, and mouth.

How do you view your child's special needs?

I see this as being able to appreciate individuality. It has been eye opening for me to be able to accept and treat every child as an individual and not just autistic. Autistic children need to be treated as though they are one of us and for people to not be so afraid because they are different. Everyone is different and everyone needs to be given a chance in life.

AGE GROUP 7-12

What would you say to other parents of special needs children just beginning their journey? What advice/suggestions would you have for them?

Listen to your gut.

Do not give up.

Engage with your child and find out what makes them happy. You are with your child 24/7 so you know what you need for your child. You are in charge and you—not anyone else—have control over the situation.

If you could think of one word to describe being a parent of a child with special needs what would it be?

Blessed.

Any final thoughts?

I would say that Mums who have been chosen to be special needs Mums are inspirational. Your child can feel you when you walk in the room; they can pick it up. They are so sensitive.

HOW DO I DO THIS?

Please list any organisations in your country that you have found helpful.

- Scope (Early Intervention services)
  https://www.scopeaust.org.au/early-years-disability-support

- I used the local council and they were great. I am now preparing for NDIS with Nathan. I have my plan and my funding and now it is a matter of finding services to put in place. Melbourne is inundated with NDIS clients and mental health clients, so paediatric psychology, psychology, and counselling are all under the pump, with an unbelievably long wait list to try to get into. Community Services is quite full on with what you see and what you hear.

- Southern Autistic School:
  https://www.southernautistic.vic.edu.au

TULIKA, RAVISH AND VEDANT (USA)

Introduction:

We are a family of four: my husband Ravish and me, our son Vedant, who is 11 and autistic (practically non-verbal) and our dog Buddy. We live in Cincinnati, Ohio, USA.

HOW DO I DO THIS?

Was it always apparent to you that your child had special needs? If not, when did you notice that something was "different" about your child?

We started noticing some delays in our son when he was around two years of age. There were red flags for autism that were getting more and more apparent as Vedant was growing.

If you have received a formal diagnosis for your child's special needs, when did this happen? Do you remember what feelings you experienced at the time and was the diagnosis a hard thing to come to terms with? Have you come to terms with it?

Our son was diagnosed around the age of three. I have no recollection of how I felt when we were handed the diagnosis. I believe I felt numb and clueless. It took us a while to come to terms with this diagnosis, although we knew in our heart that this is what it was. It was a process—from denial to grief to anger and then acceptance.

Did you research about how to help your child? What did you do? Which organisations/professionals did you reach out to?

We received a lot of help from the hospital that gave the diagnosis. They gave us a lot of resources, information, and support.

AGE GROUP 7-12

What therapies did/do you use? What routines do you find helpful for your child?

We have used quite a lot of speech and occupational therapy. Vedant has quite a lot of sensory issues, so we have integrated many sensory activities in his schedule, especially oral sensory inputs, and deep pressure.

How has having a child with special needs affected your family? Your marriage?

Having a child with special needs changed our life course. It has changed our expectations, our perspective and how we define happiness. It has also made us more sensitive and less judgmental. I believe having a special needs child does put a strain on the marriage, but that is when the strength of the bond is tested. I would like to believe that it has only made our bond stronger and our love deeper.

How do you take care of yourself? What self-care strategies do you use and how have you been able to implement them?

Even though we always must be hypervigilant with our son and that can sometimes get too tiring, I do get a chance to take a break with my friends. When our son is at school, I take time out for my hobbies. I try to stay positive as much as I can because negativity can suck the life out of you. Watching a show or a movie with my husband every now and then, while Vedant is asleep, is also very relaxing. A small chat over coffee with a good friend can also do wonders for me.

HOW DO I DO THIS?

Everything else aside, nothing rejuvenates me more than spending some quality time with Vedant. It is a common misconception that having a special needs child is all pain and tears. My house is generally filled with laughter and giggles and all of it because of our son.

Do you have a faith? If so, how has this helped you cope with life with your child?

I am not very religious, although I do believe in a higher power.

How important/necessary is your family support or the support of your friends/networks? Do you feel as though you have enough support?

It took a while for me to open up to my family and friends and educate them about our son's diagnosis and our new challenges. Once we got over that hump, we have found only support and understanding from friends and family. I have a wonderful group of friends and family members that keep me smiling and give me strength.

What do you hope/think the future holds for your child? Their living arrangements? A job? Marriage and children of their own?

Our wish for our son's future is that he is happy and content wherever he is. We wish him health, happiness, and peace. We will try our best to give him the best life possible and then leave the rest to destiny. We hope he finds a loving companion and a good quality of life—and that is all we will want for him.

AGE GROUP 7-12

What are/have been the joys of raising your child?

Our son has taught me that happiness is in the little things. While we wait for the big miracles to happen, we often overlook the little sparkles that pass right under our nose. We enjoy our son's unique personality and his company. It is a rollercoaster ride raising a child with autism, but the ride is worth every minute.

What are/have been the hardest challenges raising your child?

Our son's inability to speak is the most heartbreaking part of his disability. Although we can understand each other for the most part, there is still so much left unsaid and not understood. I wish I could know what goes on in his mind.

What has your child taught you?

Our son has given me a different perspective to life—where small victories and living in the moment are what matter. Vedant has taught me patience and persistence. He has taught me to never give up and to never give in. Every day I watch him stand up to his challenges and smile along, and it gives me so much strength just watching him go about his day.

How do you view your child's special needs?

I would be lying if I said that there is nothing that I hate about autism and that I wish Vedant did not have the challenges that he has. However, it is important to understand that not liking his diagnosis is different from not liking him. Our son is unique and has his own amazing personality that I would never want to change. I like every bit of who our son is.

What would you say to other parents of special needs children just beginning their journey? What advice/suggestions would you have for them?

Firstly, I would like to tell them that it is not their fault, so spare the guilt.

Your child is still special, with or without the diagnosis, so enjoy them and their uniqueness, rather than feel sorry for them. Be proud of them and their achievements—big or small—and be their advocate.

This is going to be a long journey and patience and persistence will get you through. Try choosing your battles. Not every battle is worth winning, so choose what you want from your child and stop comparing them with their peers. Every child grows at a different pace, so let your child grow at theirs.

If you could think of one word to describe being a parent of a child with special needs what would it be?

Inspiring.

Any final thoughts?

I always tell mothers not to try to be a supermom. It is only going to wear them out. Be gentle to yourself. Just try being there for your child and giving them every opportunity they deserve. Everything else will fall into place.

Please list any organisations in your country that you have found helpful.

- AutismSpeaks: https://www.autismspeaks.org

- Cincinnati Children's Hospital: https://www.cincinnatichildrens.org

- Autism Society of Greater Cincinnati: http://www.autismcincy.org

AGE GROUP 13-19

- Janine and Andrew, 15 (autism, sensory processing disorder, intellectual disability, and a learning disability), USA

- Lisa, John and Mark, 15 (autism and epilepsy), Australia

JANINE AND ANDREW (USA)

Introduction:

My name is Janine. My son Andrew is 15 years old and he has autism, sensory processing disorder, intellectual disability, and a learning disability. Andrew was born in New Zealand but has lived all over the world including the United States, Australia, and the Caribbean. We are currently living back in America.

HOW DO I DO THIS?

Was it always apparent to you that your child had special needs? If not, when did you notice that something was "different" about your child?

Andrew was a perfectly normal baby. He hit all his milestones up to six months of age. He was so easy, always happy, and never cried unless he was hungry or wet. When he was six months old, we travelled from New Zealand to South Carolina, USA, and Andrew got two eye infections and two ear infections on the flights.

After putting him on antibiotics, my son started to change. I joined a playgroup for him since he had no siblings. All the other children were the same age as Andrew and as time went by, I noticed that he was not doing all the things the other children were. I did worry, but everyone had a reason why to explain this—for example, he was a boy and they always talk later than girls; or he did not have any siblings to keep up with.

At one year of age, Andrew was unable to sit up on his own. We then started physical therapy and was told that some children are just born with low muscle tone. But when Andrew was three, he lost his words and by then I was extremely worried. We tried to get a correct diagnosis, but Andrew was misdiagnosed with a learning disability and advised to continue therapies and he would catch up. By age five, however, he was even further apart from other children in his development.

AGE GROUP 13-19

If you have received a formal diagnosis for your child's special needs, when did this happen? Do you remember what feelings you experienced at the time and was the diagnosis a hard thing to come to terms with? Have you come to terms with it?

Andrew was formally diagnosed with autism at the age of five. When he was earlier misdiagnosed and we were told it was not autism, I breathed a HUGE sigh of relief. When we did get the correct diagnosis, I was so sad and thought "Why me? Why him? What did I do wrong?" It took me years to accept it. The feelings were so overwhelming at times. It was so hard seeing Andrew around other children and him not being able to do what they were doing. It was super hard not being able to communicate with him and to know how he was feeling. Once I accepted that this is our new normal then things were not so hard. Acceptance is key for my sanity.

Did you research about how to help your child? What did you do? Which organisations/professionals did you reach out to?

I initially read books, specifically Jenny McCarthy's books about her son: *"Louder Than Words: A Mother's Journey in Healing Autism"*, *"Healing and Preventing Autism: A Complete Guide"* and *"Mother Warriors: A Nation of Parents Healing Autism Against All Odds"*.

I literally read her second book in one day and kept saying "This is Andrew!!!" I did not even wait for the diagnosis but changed my son's diet that day. We eliminated all gluten, casein, soy, and anything artificial (colours, sweeteners, and flavours). I dove in and read every book I could get my hands on—for example, books on sensory processing and how to toilet train special needs children—you name it, I read it!

HOW DO I DO THIS?

At the time we lived in Hilton Head Island, South Carolina, USA. We had a local organization called the Low Country Autism Society and they were a great resource for me. I also made friends with other parents with children on the spectrum and they were a great resource of information and support. We started speech, physical and occupational therapies. We wanted to do ABA but were unable to do so for a while.

After going to numerous paediatricians and having my heart broken by being told "This is how your child is, just deal with it, he will never get better or change" we found a wonderful DAN! (Defeat Autism Now!) doctor who was a great help. He understood Andrew's special needs and what testing we should do. We did Heavy Metal testing, OAT test (Organic Acid Test), food sensitivity tests and nutritional deficiency testing. These gave us a game plan to help with Andrew's health.

What therapies did/do you use? What routines do you find helpful for your child?

Andrew has been in occupational, physical and speech therapies since he was a baby/toddler, and all of these have helped to an extent. We have also undertaken music therapy and hippotherapy (horseback riding).

We are ALL about routine!! When that routine is disrupted is when things go wrong.

How has having a child with special needs affected your family? Your marriage?

My siblings and parents were always very supportive, but they just do not understand a lot. They try to help, but sometimes it is frustrating how they just do not GET it! My husband had a hugely difficult time with Andrew's diagnosis. He could not understand that when Andrew was loud it was just him being him, and Daddy would tell him to "Be quiet". He also could not accept that Andrew was not "normal". We tried, but after almost 20 years of marriage I left my husband and brought Andrew back to America from Australia. It was the BEST move I could have made. Andrew was unable to receive any support for his disability because he was not an Australian citizen, but now in America he is getting all the therapies and support he so desperately needed!

How do you take care of yourself? What self-care strategies do you use and how have you been able to implement them?

I make sure I have a massage at least once a month and a facial every 6-8 weeks. I meditate daily and hit the gym or do some sort of exercise at least four times a week. Getting a good sweat on and the heart rate going helps with stress!! I have something fun planned just for myself at least once a week—coffee with a friend, drinks and dinner or a movie out.

I meet once a week with my "tribe" to mastermind, grow and learn. I am fortunate to have started on a Superfood Nutritional program called Isagenix. We started for our health and had such amazing results that I told everyone I knew about it. EVERY single teacher, aid and therapist saw a difference in Andrew within the first couple of weeks. Next thing you know I was building a business!! I have not been able to work because Andrew is my full-time job, but now I am able to support us as well, all by helping others with their health.

HOW DO I DO THIS?

Do you have a faith? If so, how has this helped you cope with life with your child?

I was raised Catholic, but I have not attended church since my Mom's funeral ten years ago. However, I consider myself extremely spiritual. I do not think I need to have a faith and go to church to believe in God/Source/Universe. I am way more spiritual now that I have my son than I ever was before. It has helped me because I am able to pray/meditate for peace. I know I am just a very small piece of the bigger picture.

How important/necessary is your family support or the support of your friends/networks? Do you feel as though you have enough support?

As much as I dearly love my close family, they just do not understand what life is like for us. I am very appreciative of all their love and support, but it is not enough. I do have extended support groups with other parents who have become friends. I moved last year, and I am still making new friends and finding a place that we "belong". I just recently joined a support group and boy, oh boy did it come along at the right time!! It is wonderful to be able to attend with others who understand, and to vent, cry or whatever without any judgment.

What do you hope/think the future holds for your child? Their living arrangements? A job? Marriage and children of their own?

Because of my son's intellectual disability and his autism, I cannot see any sort of paying job, marriage, and children of his own in the future. I do see Andrew volunteering somewhere that has to do with animals. I am hoping that once he is done with school, he will be able to move into some sort of group home with others like him.

What are/have been the joys of raising your child?

I experience pure joy every time I see Andrew smile. It has not been easy, but I love him more than life itself. I would do anything under the sun to help him. He will forever be a young person inside an adult body. He will forever be innocent with a heart and soul purer than anything else.

What are/have been the hardest challenges raising your child?

It has been hard not being able to have a conversation with Andrew or hear him say "I love you Momma". It is a hard challenge not always knowing exactly what is going on inside his head—is he scared, anxious, happy, sad? Even though he is non-verbal, my son does tell me he loves me in so many ways.

What has your child taught you?

Andrew has taught me many things, but I think the biggest is to slow down and smell the flowers. He will, literally, still do this and it does not need to be a flower; it could be a stick or even a leaf off a tree. I think that Mother Earth needs us all to slow down and take a good look at what is going on around us and how we are treating our planet and fellow humankind.

HOW DO I DO THIS?

I am more resilient now. I remember worrying about what people would say or how they would look at us in public; now I just simply do not care. I am not shy to stand up for him or to politely educate anyone. Awareness is key.

I have been Andrew's biggest cheerleader and will continue to be so until the day I die.

How do you view your child's special needs?

I must admit, it is so darn hard sometimes, just wishing Andrew could do things other children could do. Recently we tried basketball with Special Olympics. The sensory overload was so bad Andrew literally put me in a bear hug and hit me in the head a dozen times before I could get him off me. This is a super sweet child who loves everyone—a complete baby and animal whisperer. I felt so sad in that moment, not for Andrew, but for the child he would never be.

What would you say to other parents of special needs children just beginning their journey? What advice/suggestions would you have for them?

I would say to learn to accept your child as they are. Do not listen to all the doctors, as they are not gods and do not know everything. You will know your child better than anyone else. Do not let anyone else tell you what is best for your child. You are their parent and that unconditional love will keep your aim true. Listen to your gut, it is never EVER wrong. Make friends with other families as they will be a great support when you need it.

AGE GROUP 13-19

Get the diagnosis so you can get the help your child needs. Do not be afraid to ask for help when you need it. Take care of YOU so you can take care of them.

Make sure you keep your child healthy! This is HUGE. I see so many parents feed their child junk food, soda and the like and that will just lead to disease—and who needs more things to deal with?

If you could think of one word to describe being a parent of a child with special needs what would it be?

Warrior Mom, without a doubt. Who else can deal with getting vomited on in the middle of the night while consoling their child it will be okay? Who else can keep their cool under the worst of situations, having to give enemas so their child can have a bowel movement, change nappies for over a decade, buy all organic foods and cook everything from scratch so their child can get the best nutrition possible, smash tablets and open capsules to create a drink with all this goodness and probiotics to help boost their immune system? Who else would drive hours to appointments to go to the best specialist/homeopath/naturopath and go without, so my child can have what he needs?

I spend hours every week in the waiting room of therapy sessions (occupational, physical, speech and music therapy—you name it!), but I just do it, because I am a Warrior Mom and I love my son.

Any final thoughts?

I cannot wait to read the book!

HOW DO I DO THIS?

Please list any organisations in your country that you have found helpful.

In the USA:

- LAF Lowcountry Autism Foundation in Hilton Head, SC, USA: www.lafinc.org

- Heroes on Horseback Hippotherapy in Hilton Head, SC, USA: https://www.heroesonhorseback.org/

- Autism Society of Greater Phoenix, AZ, USA https://phxautism.org

In New Zealand:

- RDA Riding for the Disabled Hippotherapy, Whangarei, New Zealand: http://rdawhangarei.org.nz

Isagenix:

- To contact Janine about Isagenix please email her at: TransformWithIsa@gmail.com

LISA, JOHN AND MARK (AUSTRALIA)

Introduction:

My name is Lisa Futer and I live with my husband John and our son Mark on some rural acreage in Townsville, Queensland, Australia. Mark is 15 and he is non-verbal with severe autism and epilepsy.

Mark attends Townsville Community Learning Centre (TCLC)[12] which is a special school for children with disabilities.

---

[12] https://tclcspecs.eq.edu.au accessed June 2020

HOW DO I DO THIS?

Was it always apparent to you that your child had special needs? If not, when did you notice that something was "different" about your child?

Mark was developing typically until he was around 14 months of age. His development regressed and he lost eye contact and any speech.

Because I am a special needs teacher, I picked up some of these signs sooner than I may have. My husband did not believe there was a problem and thought that I had been in special education for too long.

If you have received a formal diagnosis for your child's special needs, when did this happen? Do you remember what feelings you experienced at the time and was the diagnosis a hard thing to come to terms with? Have you come to terms with it?

Mark was around two when we received the diagnosis of autism. My Dad and I had to go to Brisbane to a specialist centre to get the diagnosis as doctors were reluctant to give a diagnosis to a child who was so young.

I remember feeling totally alone and not really knowing where to turn. Because my husband was in denial, it was difficult to discuss this with him. I was also angry. Different feelings came in waves and I could not understand why this was happening to us. I had a healthy pregnancy and I did everything by the book. We had a loving home for Mark, and he was very much wanted.

It was a hard thing to come to terms with and I still grieve at certain milestones that are not met or which Mark has yet to face.

AGE GROUP 13-19

Did you research about how to help your child? What did you do? Which organisations/professionals did you reach out to?

We researched everything on autism including alternative therapies. Initially, we were looking for a cure. We looked at naturopathies and dietary interventions. We were even going to do stem cell treatment[13].

Mark had early intervention initially with the Department of Education and then attended AEIOU[14] and did Applied Behavioural Analysis (ABA)[15]. We had a consultation with Professor Tony Attwood at Minds and Hearts[16] in Brisbane, as well as speech and occupational therapies. We attended whatever courses were available—for example, sensory processing training.

What therapies did/do you use? What routines do you find helpful for your child?

From the beginning we went to speech therapy and this made a really big difference to Mark. He was able to communicate using Facilitated Communication (where he was supported to type on a keyboard), and it gave us an insight into what Mark was thinking and feeling. Mark has had the same speech therapist now for nine years and so he responds to her extremely well.

---

[13] https://www.choice.com.au/health-and-body/hospitals-and-medical-procedures/medical-treatments/articles/stem-cell-therapy

[14]

[15] https://www.verywellhealth.com/aba-applied-behavioral-analysis-therapy-autism-259913

[16] Dr Michelle Garnett and Professor Tony Attwood, leading world authorities on Autism Spectrum Disorder, are part of the clinical team and provide clinical supervision at Minds and Hearts. https://mindsandhearts.net all above accessed June 2020

HOW DO I DO THIS?

We use occupational therapy and find that this is helpful, but it takes a while to find the right person who can then be able to build up a rapport with Mark. Mark has been with a male occupational therapist for the past six months, and so they are still building a relationship. He seems to understand autism and is very patient with Mark, knowing when to push—and when not to. It also depends on how Mark is on the day as to whether he will participate.

Mark loves swimming, which calms him and helps with his sensory issues. Unfortunately, he is unable to do this at present because of grommets[17] in his ears.

Mark does not like change; he likes routine. He uses the PODD (Pragmatic Organisation Dynamic Display)[18] system to communicate, using aided symbols such as pictures, graphic symbols, and whole written words. This allows Mark to choose what he would like to do and to articulate how he is feeling. School holidays are harder for Mark; he gets bored, but he has been reluctant to want to go out during this last holidays. Usually he does better once he is back at school and this year, he started senior school in a new area with new teachers. This was a huge challenge for all of us and I dreaded it because even though we spoke to Mark about the change he thought he was going back to the same class with the same teacher he has been with for three years.

I think the thing about having a special needs child is that they are constantly surprising you. As a parent, I find that I often underestimate Mark. This is what happened when Mark started back at school this

---

[17] Grommets are tiny tubes that are inserted into the eardrum to drain fluid. They are used after repeated ear infections that can cause 'glue ear'. They are inserted during minor surgery but under general anaesthetic and they usually fall out naturally after 6-12 months. https://www.healthdirect.gov.au/grommets

[18] http://www.spectronics.com.au/product/pragmatic-organisation-dynamic-display-podd-communication-books-direct-access-templates all accessed June 2020

year. Apart from a brief unsettled period, Mark has coped so well and is really enjoying his new class.

How has having a child with special needs affected your family? Your marriage?

This has had a huge impact on my marriage, especially in the early days. Instead of bringing us closer together, my husband and I seemed to take the stress out on each other. Now our relationship is a lot stronger and we work together to solve any issues that arise.

My parents never said a lot as they wanted to protect us, but I have no doubt that they grieved and struggled to accept the diagnosis. However, they were an amazing support both physically and emotionally and would drop everything to come and help us. My Mum started a support group for parents with children with autism called the Teapot Club in Goulburn NSW[19]. It started with a couple of friends and instead of going out for coffee, they would meet at each other's houses and put some money in the teapot for autism. They do an amazing job and provide education and funding to help families with autistic children in their area. Last year Mum was nominated for Goulburn's Australian of the Year for her work in the Teapot Club.

---

[19] https://www.goulburnpost.com.au/story/3521164/teapot-club-topped-up-by-cafe/ accessed June 2020

HOW DO I DO THIS?

How do you take care of yourself? What self-care strategies do you use and how have you been able to implement them?

I am still working on this and I am trying to make this a priority, but due to Mark's poor sleeping habits my husband and I do not get much sleep. I am aware that I need to take care of myself, but it is so much easier said than done.

I like to meet friends for coffee and occasionally go away. I try and get a massage every few months and I get manicures and pedicures.

My husband and I try and go out for lunch when we have respite for Mark.

Do you have a faith? If so, how has this helped you cope with life with your child?

I do have a faith and it has given me the strength to face the challenges that arise in all areas of life.

How important/necessary is your family support or the support of your friends/networks? Do you feel as though you have enough support?

Support from family and friends is extremely important. Being able to network with likeminded people who understand what it is like to have a child with a disability—most of my friends have children with special needs—is invaluable.

Wider organisations such as Carers Queensland have provided emotional support in the form of retreats, pampering days and social get togethers, as well as counselling, and they have been able to put me in touch with likeminded people.

Mark has up to two carers who take him to school and pick him up each day. This has made a big difference to our lives as it has allowed me to work. Mark also has support every Saturday and goes to a respite house once a month for two nights. All of this comes through NDIS, as well as funding for occupational and speech therapies and behaviour management, which has made a big difference—financially and emotionally—for our family. It allows John and I to have some time to ourselves.

We are grateful for the support we get, and while I feel it is enough, we still get extremely tired, because of Mark's lack of sleep.

What do you hope/think the future holds for your child? Their living arrangements? A job? Marriage and children of their own?

I lay awake at night worrying about what the future holds when John and I are no longer around. However, I try not to dwell on this and hope that the things we put in place for Mark will give him the most independent and content life possible.

That is why we hope to have Mark in some form of assisted accommodation sooner rather than later. We are hoping to begin this transition when he leaves school and becomes a young adult. This is important to us as we would like to see him settled while we are still able to take an active role in this. We have a house ready for Mark when the time comes, and our plan and hope is to find enough support workers to provide 24/7 support for him.

HOW DO I DO THIS?

I would like to see Mark as independent as possible and, like any parent, my greatest wish is for Mark to be happy. At this stage I do not see a job in his future but who knows what the future holds? I have seen Mark make great strides—but then there are some days he will not leave the house or get out of the car. It is hard because you want these things for them, but Mark faces so many challenges daily, I wonder what is possible.

I feel the same about the possibility of marriage and children for Mark.

What are/have been the joys of raising your child?

Mark is a happy and cheeky child who does not have a mean bone in his body and wants everybody to be happy. When Mark is laughing and engaging with us, everything else melts away. He really is an amazing and inspirational young man. It might be a cliché, but I would not change places for the world.

Mark keeps persevering no matter what challenges he faces, and it is always an achievement when he reaches a milestone that has been difficult previously.

What are/have been the hardest challenges raising your child?

The biggest challenge is the meltdowns. As a parent, it is so difficult to stand by and watch as your child hurts themselves and sometimes others. This never gets easier and there is nothing you can do to stop your child hurting themselves.

Mark usually displays "whispers" (signs that show he is getting stressed) before a meltdown. For example, he will flap his hands and maybe bite his hand. At this stage, we must make sure everyone is safe. The dogs are put outside as Mark will bite them (not the other way around). Mark will then start biting himself, throwing himself on the ground and bashing his head and he will also try to bite or attack anyone who is near him.

Through experience, we have found that if we try to hold Mark or intervene this makes things escalate, so now we find if we go to a different room right out of Mark's space he will calm down quicker. Mark told us to do this using Facilitated Communication where he typed, "You people are annoying, you need to leave me alone and go upstairs and just leave me alone". So, we respected his wishes and things have certainly become easier because of this.

If we are in the car and Mark has a meltdown it is a little bit more difficult as it is in a confined space. As Mark can still hurt us, we make sure that he is safe and then we stand outside of the car next to where we can see Mark. He calms down quicker when we are out of the car and he can get whatever is troubling him out of his system.

Another challenge is Mark's lack of sleep, although this is much better than it used to be—in the early days he would sleep three hours a night. Now Mark sleeps from 10 or 11 pm until 6 am most nights, but at least two nights a week he may be up all night or get up at 3 or 4 in the morning.

Mark is gluten free and his diet is really limited, with no fruit or vegetables. If Mark sees or smells a banana, he will be sick. Over the years we have tried everything to get him to eat more, including hiding vegetables in his meals, but he would know straight away. He eats gluten-free bread, gluten-free chicken nuggets, crackers, potato chips, chicken, and French fries—all white foods. He is not able to drink water; he drinks apple and blackcurrant cordial.

HOW DO I DO THIS?

What has your child taught you?

Mark has taught me patience and resilience. I figure if Mark can deal with all the obstacles he has to endure and keep going, then so can I.

How do you view your child's special needs?

There are many ups and downs that come with having a child with autism.

Sometimes I have a false sense of security that everything is okay when things are going well and Mark is happy and content, but in reality, I am just waiting for the next unpredictable and challenging behaviour. I do try to enjoy the good times and my time with Mark.

What would you say to other parents of special needs children just beginning their journey? What advice/suggestions would you have for them?

I would say take one day at a time. Trust your instincts as you know your child best. You are stronger than you think you are.

If you could think of one word to describe being a parent of a child with special needs what would it be?

Proud.

I am so incredibly proud of my boy, with what he copes with.

AGE GROUP 13-19

Any final thoughts?

Medication has helped Mark. It has been trial and error and right now he is on Risperidone and Lamictal[20] for mood and with seizures and this is going well. Mark has not had a tonic clonic seizure[21] for quite some time although he is still having absence seizures[22]. We have an amazing GP who has a great rapport with Mark. Sometimes if Mark refuses to get out of the car when he has an appointment to see him, this wonderful doctor will come out to the car to see Mark.

Please list any organisations in your country that you have found helpful.

- Townsville Community Learning Centre – A State Special School. https://tclcspecs.eq.edu.au

- Minds and Hearts is a private clinic led by Dr David Zimmerman and Dr Wesley Turner, Clinical Psychologists. The clinic, located in Brisbane, Queensland, Australia, was founded by Dr Michelle Garnett in 2005 to meet the enormous need for Allied Health Services specifically tailored for people on the Autism Spectrum, and to increase knowledge and awareness of autism. https://mindsandhearts.net

- AEIOU Foundation for children with autism has nine centres across Queensland and one in Adelaide, South Australia. https://aeiou.org.au

---

[20] https://www.healthdirect.gov.au/medicines/brand/amt,4438011000036105/lamictal

[21] https://www.epilepsy.com/learn/types-seizures/tonic-clonic-seizures

[22] https://www.epilepsy.com/learn/types-seizures/absence-seizures all accessed June 2020

HOW DO I DO THIS?

- The National Disability Insurance Scheme https://www.ndis.gov.au The NDIS gives all Australians peace of mind if they, their child or loved one is born with or acquires a permanent and significant disability, they will get the support they need. The NDIS is not a welfare system but is designed to help people get the support they need so their skills and independence improve over time.

- Carers Queensland https://carersqld.com.au

AGE GROUP 20-30

- Diane, Jerry, Lena, Ian and Jolene, 21 (high-functioning autism), USA

- Ruth and Emily, 22 (high-functioning autism), Australia

- Teresa, Graeme, Joseph and Sarah, 23 (high-functioning autism, ODD, OCD, expressive/receptive language disorder), Australia

- William, Sandra and Nowell, 23 (Prader-Willi Syndrome), Australia

- Deborah, Colin, Ryan and Andrew, 24 (autism), United Kingdom

- Gabriella and Jordan, 24 (autism, Fragile X, intellectual impairment), Australia

- Meredith and Sarah, 25 (autism, sensory processing disorder, PTSD, epilepsy), Australia

DIANE, JERRY, LENA, IAN AND JOLENE (USA)

Introduction

We are a family of five—I am Diane, there's my husband Jerry, our son Ian, 25 and our daughter Jolene, 21. I also have another daughter, Lena, who was born before I met Jerry. We live in a little town called Burton, Michigan, in the USA. We are not too far from Flint, the site of the water system lead contamination crisis of 2014[23].

Jolene is high-functioning autistic.

---

[23] https://www.npr.org/sections/thetwo-way/2016/04/20/465545378/lead-laced-water-in-flint-a-step-by-step-look-at-the-makings-of-a-crisis accessed June 2020

HOW DO I DO THIS?

Was it always apparent to you that your child had "special needs"? If not, when did you first notice that something was "different" about your child?

After we had Jolene, we noticed she was not meeting her milestones—she was not rolling over or sitting up. Just before she turned one, Jolene quit sucking her bottle—so we had to buy a flexible one, make the nipple hole big enough and squeeze the milk into her mouth.

When Jolene was two, she would walk on her knees and not on her feet. She was talking, but then she stopped. When she was placed in her first special needs class, none of the children spoke. Jolene had begun learning sign language and then she was transferred to another class where many of the children spoke. Suddenly, she started talking again—almost nonstop … LOL! We were unsure as to why—it could have been the prayer at church or being in a class with other kids who talked—or a combination of both. Back then, Jolene would have a monologue with herself, especially at night after we put her to bed. She still does this, and she also likes to have chats with both her dad and me about her day.

Jolene had also had her first febrile seizure[24] at age two and again when she was four. This last one went for approximately ten minutes and Jolene was so exhausted by it she was out for hours—thankfully, that was the last one she ever had.

We think our son Ian might also be Asperger's, but he was always able to get by in school. We did not want to label him, and we thought it was good if he could get by and if he needed extra help along the way, we would do this. Ian was spelling and sounding out words (reading) at age

---

[24] Febrile seizures are convulsions in children, usually under the age of five, caused by elevated body temperatures.
https://www.rch.org.au/kidsinfo/fact_sheets/Febrile_Convulsions

three and doing math problems designed for those twice his age. His favourite movie/book was Dr Seuss *"ABC – An Amazing Alphabet Book!"* and he loved Matchbox cars, but they had to have numbers on them, as did his shirts. He would wear them backwards because he had to have the numbers showing in the front where he could see them.

If you have received a formal diagnosis for your child's special needs, when did this happen? Do you remember what feelings you experienced at the time, and was the diagnosis a hard thing to come to terms with? Have you come to terms with it?

When Jolene was around two years of age, we took her to a paediatrician who referred her to a paediatric neurologist. At first he thought she had Rett Syndrome[25] (this is a rare genetic mutation affecting brain development in girls), but he figured it wasn't this because girls with Rett lack the physical ability to smile—and Jolene was a real happy baby. So, the diagnosis she was given was autism.

I was crushed when I found out. I was by myself; Jerry was at work. My sister works with special needs kids in an adult centre and so I stopped by to talk to her because I needed someone who understood. When your child is born, you have dreams for them and then all of a sudden it's like someone came and took a big eraser and erased it all away and you are forced to start from scratch all over again.

Luckily, we were going to a church and we had our faith.

We think we have now come to terms with our daughter's diagnosis; it was just a matter of getting our mindset to a different level. We try not to treat Jolene as special and we have tried to discipline her along the

---

[25] www.webmd.com/brain/autism/rett-syndrome all accessed June 2020

same lines as her brother Ian. We have not purposely tried to treat her differently, but it is hard because she *is* different.

Did you research about how to help your child? What did you do? Which organisations/professionals did you reach out to?

We got early intervention for Jolene and later, once I got more into using the computer, I would research autism related topics to help us understand it better. We have always had help from my sister Lori and her son Scott, as well as my elder daughter, who have all been trained to work with special needs people.

Jolene attended various schools in and around Flint Michigan. The teachers were amazing; they loved their kids, were incredibly involved with them and were able to give Jolene a lot of support. At one stage Jolene attended Barhitte Elementary School[26], the same school as her brother Ian. Her class was made up of at least 20 or more children, with a diversity of special needs. Jolene had been used to a smaller class of 10 and under, and so this was not ideal for her and did not work out well.

Jolene is now attending the Transition Center[27], where she receives training in life/work skills, to help her adapt to adult life should she ever want to work.

We do not really go to a lot of autism groups or anything. Jolene likes to be on her Kindle, listening to music or watching TV, and has not really expressed the need to be more social.

---

[26] http://bentley.ss5.sharpschool.com/schools/barhitte_elementary

[27] https://www.geneseeisd.org/educational_programs/special_education/transition_center all accessed June 2020

AGE GROUP 20-30

What therapies did/do you use? What routines do you find helpful for your child?

Jolene got a lot of occupational and physical therapy when she was younger; some of this was at school and some at a regular medical building where they would also work with her speech.

For a while we had to blend all Jolene's food—otherwise, she would not eat. It was almost like she had a taste where she did not like whole foods. She does not like ice-cream but will drink ice slushie drinks.

We were taught how to do joint compressions[28] which were extremely helpful, and we would massage Jolene with lavender oils. We also got her a swing and a mini trampoline, but she was not really interested in either.

How has having a child with special needs affected your family? Your marriage? Your other children?

Our family life has not been affected by Jolene's special needs—they have been something we have accepted and dealt with. Our marriage has not really been affected either. Before we got married, the pastor who was marrying us had us take a "compatibility test" of sorts and Jerry and I found our views on child raising were similar. Jerry loves kids and adapted to Jolene's special needs very well. He treats her like a princess anyways and is a soft touch; I am the one who has to be the bad guy.

Lena, my elder daughter, was not affected as she was 20 and had already left home when I had Jolene. She was also special needs trained. In

---

[28] Joint compression promotes self-organisation and improves attention span of an autistic child. It almost covers major skill developments.
https://chicagooccupationaltherapy.com/articles/how-joint-compressions accessed June 2020.

HOW DO I DO THIS?

some ways, Jolene having special needs helped us to recognise our son Ian was also on the autism spectrum. When we were researching for Jolene, we came across some things which also applied to Ian—an aversion to loud noises, smelling foods and poor social skills. He has never had good eye contact but is currently working on making his social skills better.

How do you take care of yourself? What self-care strategies do you use and how have you been able to implement them?

Back in 2013, when Ian graduated from High School, my husband and I decided to splurge and buy me my first really nice camera—a Nikon. Photography has always been really relaxing for me and if worse comes to worst, I can get in the car, go to the nature reserve, and walk around taking pictures.

I like being on the computer and I belong to a game site called Club Pogo which has a lot of different games like card games, question games, and Bingo. I have always loved to read, and I watch crime shows like *C.S.I.* on TV, as well as romance, classic television shows (like *The Waltons, Little House on the Prairie* and *M*A*S*H*), home improvement shows and comedy. I also like a good psychological horror movie like Alfred Hitchcock's *"The Birds"* or *"Psycho"*.

Do you have a faith? If so, how has this helped you cope with life with your child?

Yes, I have always had a faith. I grew up in Protestant and Southern Baptist churches, but as an adult, I no longer felt comfortable in that kind of church. I had kind of drifted away from my faith before I met my husband Jerry. I was attracted to him because he had such a deep faith; he also loved children. We started going to church, most of them charismatic and non-denominational, with praise and worship, sung to contemporary Christian songs. I had our son Ian when I was 36 and I was almost 40 when Jerry and I got married—Jolene was born the following year.

Our faith has been a major part of keeping us together as a solid family. We have always turned to God and Jerry prays with Jolene every night—this is Jerry and Jolene's father/daughter time. At church, we take Jolene up for prayer and they pray over her.

I believe God only gives special kids to special parents who can handle it. I was honoured that He chose us as these kinds of people, and I do not want to let Him down.

How important/necessary is your family support or the support of your friends/networks? Do you feel as though you have enough support?

My sister and nephew are supportive, as is my elder daughter Lena—even though she now lives in Wyoming.

Every church we have attended has always been so supportive of Jolene. For example, she has a fascination with lotions and perfumes, like Bath 'n Body Works. She cannot always go there, so people at church were always bringing them to her. This eventually had to stop because Jolene had bins and bins of them! She loves the perfume samples and the fashion pictures in magazines as well as anything that catches her eye to put in her as yet non-existent scrapbook. When she was little, she liked the feel of the paper. She would be in her crib and she would shred paper up, like a baby hamster in a nest.

HOW DO I DO THIS?

I feel that I have enough support. Friends and family (on Jerry's side as well) have always been wonderful with Jolene, keeping an eye out for her. No-one in the family has ever been anything but supportive—Jolene is a loved little lady. My Dad just adored her. Before he died, he was worried how the world would be for her as she got older. It upset him to think someone would be cruel to her and treat her like she was stupid or mentally challenged.

What do you hope/think the future holds for your child? Their living arrangements? A job? Marriage and children of their own?

We believe Jolene might eventually get some part-time work, but we do not think she will be living on her own. She knows basic skills like using the microwave and pouring her own cereal, but she does need help with ADLs (activities of daily living skills—everyday personal care activities), like brushing her teeth and washing her hair. Sometimes she puts her clothes on inside out and backwards and we help her with that. She does not wear tie-up shoes—only slip on shoes—but sometimes she puts them on the wrong feet.

We cannot see Jolene dating and being married; she has never really expressed a big interest in that. As parents, we do not know how we would feel; we would hate to see her getting into something we were not there to look after. We have always cared for her in a certain way and if she were away from us, we would have to be comfortable with the situation—knowing she was loved and not being mistreated.

Jolene receives Social Security. We would leave her the house and stipulate either someone live with her, or else hire someone that could come in for room and board and a small wage to care for her. That is a big fear of ours; especially during this virus (COVID 19). It is scary to think that Jerry or I could be gone—just like that. We have already made our son a back-up guardian in case something should ever happen to us, but we do not know if our son is emotionally and financially ready to take on caring for his sister. My other daughter has the training and so we always have her there to step in.

I also found out I am diabetic, as well as having high blood pressure and I need to watch my health with that. It is a scary thing, but life goes on and you just deal with it.

What are/have been the joys of raising your child?

Jolene is such a loving person. I remember when she was little, and we would be at the doctors' offices where she would go up to all the ladies in the waiting room and tell them they were pretty. She would make their day. We called her our little goodwill ambassador, and, in this way, she is just like my Dad, who used to say, "There are no strangers in our life; only friends we have yet to make". As she got older, due to the threat of child abduction, paedophiles and molesters, we would have to tell Jolene "You can't do that if Mom or Daddy aren't around; you just can't go up to people you don't know and give them hugs and kisses unless we say it's okay".

As a rule, she is easy going and funny and very rarely gets angry, but when she does, she can get out of control. Jolene can be quite creative with her ensembles and does not want me to help her pick out what clothes to wear anymore. If her clothes are clean and neat, I say let her go with it, as she has the right to dress herself. Sometimes I send her back in to change to just probably tone things down a little, because it hurts Mama's eyes.

HOW DO I DO THIS?

There is never a dull moment with Jolene; she keeps us on our toes! Kids can make you feel either really young or really old—and Jolene does both.

What are/have been the hardest challenges raising your child?

Overall, the challenges have been quite low key. The main one has been just worrying about people taking advantage of her. Jolene is a pretty girl who developed quite early and was/is quite innocent. We live in a park with modular homes in a good-sized community of 200-300 people. There are lots of walking spaces and we see kids walking around by themselves, but we cannot allow Jolene to do that by herself. We feel bad about this, but we worry that there might be some bad people out there who would take advantage of her, hurt her—or worse.

We also find it a challenge to try to get Jolene to fit into the dynamics of life and to work out how she can do things that a lot of people might not think she can do. It is also hard to see her not having those "normal" friendships where she has friends come over, or go to parties and sleepovers, or get on the phone and text and yak. That is a hard challenge, because all parents want their kids to have a big social circle and be accepted and be a part of things. But it is what it is. Jolene gets invited for sleepovers by her cousins or other relatives who are near her age. Occasionally she would go to the movies with her school, but she is not big on this, as she has neither the interest nor the attention span to sit and watch all the way through.

AGE GROUP 20-30

What has your child taught you?

Jolene has taught me to be more patient. I have never been a real patient person—maybe it is my Scottish heritage as we tend to go off the deep end quicker than some other nationalities. My Dad was like that and so I am not sure if this is nature or nurture.

Jolene has taught us to take things slower and to try to gear our discipline and interactions with her more than we would if she were— and I hate to use this word— "normal". She has taught us to appreciate life and to stop and realise not to take things for granted. Most especially she has taught us that EVERYONE deserves to be loved and treated with respect!

How do you view your child's special needs?

We would be lying to ourselves if we said there were not things to overcome every day, but we also embrace Jolene's uniqueness. She is her own person. Kids that are not autistic get to a certain age and try to emulate others and want to be just like them, with wearing certain clothes and so on. But Jolene does not have that—and I do not think she even realises that she is not wanting to be like that. This makes our lives easier because we do not have to worry about her experimenting with drugs, smoking or drinking, or being in places she should not be.

I raised my elder daughter as a single mother. She was not a bad kid, but she was a normal teenager wanting to experiment and try things out and I had to come down hard on her a few times. I know that being a parent of a teenager is not always the most pleasant thing, but you both survive it and come out the other side for the better. With Jolene, I never have those worries. Maybe I am sticking my head in the sand saying I don't see it so it is not there, but it is a kind of relief having one set of issues that I wouldn't have to deal with had Jolene not had autism.

HOW DO I DO THIS?

What would you say to other parents of special needs children just beginning their journey? What advice/suggestions would you have for them?

If you have already been told to get intervention for your child, then as soon as possible get them into a good school with a good program. This made all the difference for Jolene. It's like the saying about teaching the old dog new tricks; the earlier you can get them into some sort of program working with all the aspects of autism—occupational, physical, mental—the easier you can begin to retrain their thought patterns. Let your child evolve at their own pace. If you set your expectations too high, you are just going to make the both of you frustrated and set up for disappointment. Your child needs to be who they are, and you just need to learn to make life as easy for the both of you as possible.

I do not think you should spoil or cushion your child just because they are "different", because what if something happened to you and you were not there anymore? It would be harder for them. Let them know they are no better or worse than their siblings—or anyone else for that matter—and that there are rules and consequences (for example, Jolene can lose the use of her Kindle or CD player for at least 24 hours or more) for their bad decisions and actions, as well as rewards for good ones.

If you could think of one word to describe being a parent of a child with special needs what would it be?

Adventurous! Part of being autistic is that, even though they like the sameness, they are never the same. You never know what they are going to say or do—for example, you could be out in public and they can embarrass you or do something to make you so proud. There is never a dull moment—and we can never "sleep" on the job!

When Jolene was younger, she was not a good sleeper and her first bedroom had a Dutch door (a regular door cut in half horizontally in the middle) with the top half left open so we could hear her at night. We had to move the lock and install it on the bottom half of the door, because when the lock was at the top, Jolene learned that if she put her toybox next to it, she could stand on it and unlock the door. Another time at church, her Sunday School teacher (my sister) told the kids that if they misbehaved, they would have to go back to their parents. So, Jolene slapped her aunty and said "There, take me upstairs to my Mom and Dad." My sister gave Jolene a couple of smacks on the bottom for inappropriate behaviour and then she had her come back into the classroom instead of going upstairs to us. People think autism goes with stupidity but that is not true; Jolene is just slower in learning normal things.

It is always an adventure with Jolene. She does not run a true pattern.

Any final thoughts?

Jolene is just a unique person and that is the upside of autism; they are so unique. There is never a mould they fit into; one day they can be one way and the next day they can be completely different. They do not stick in a pattern for long and they are always changing up the game. She has taught us, as trite as it sounds, to "stop and smell the roses" and really appreciate some of the smaller and insignificant things in life.

HOW DO I DO THIS?

Please list any organisations in your country that you have found helpful.

Schools:

- Reid Elementary School, Goodrich, Michigan https://res.goodrichschools.org/

- Genesee ISD Childhood Programs and Services, Flint, Michigan https://www.geneseeisd.org/educational_programs/special_education/ecps

- Friel Street Elementary School, Burton, Michigan

- Perry Elementary School, Grand Blanc, Michigan https://www.niche.com/k12/perry-innovation-center--and--upper-school-grand-blanc-mic /

- Brendel Elementary School, Grand Blanc, Michigan, http://brendel-elementary-school.grandblanc.schoolblocks.com/

- Grand Blanc High School, Grand Blanc, Michigan (Middle School) https://www.gbcs.org/hs

- Carman-Ainsworth High School, Flint Michigan (High School) https://www.carman.k12.mi.us

- Transition Center, Flint, Michigan at https://www.geneseeisd.org/educational_programs/special_education/transition_center

- The Internet

- Having family and friends who either have children that are autistic or who work with children with autism.

AGE GROUP 20-30

Churches:

- Mount Hope Church, Grand Blanc, Michigan
  https://www.mhcgb.com

- Hill Creek Church, Swartz Creek, Michigan
  https://hillcreekchurch.org

RUTH AND EMILY (AUSTRALIA)

Introduction:

Hi, my name is Ruth Groundwater. I am 52 years young and have three wonderful children: Harvey 24, Emily Phaedra 22, and Joel 21. We currently live in Townsville, Queensland, Australia. Since our separation in 2010, the children's father, Carl, has not been around for many years.

Emily has progressed up the autism chart and is now high functioning autistic, with intellectual disabilities, and the emotional maturity age of a 10- to 12-year-old.

AGE GROUP 20-30

Was it always apparent to you that your child had special needs? If not, when did you notice that something was "different" about your child?

When Em was born, we lived in outback Kununurra, Queensland. No-one ever said anything, but there were a couple of things that did not feel right—for example, her eyes appeared to be different shapes with one more oblong than the other; also, the soft part of the skull that closes did so very quickly (the nurse made notes about this).

Em was the most perfect baby, with such a gentle touch. She would wake in the morning and, rather than cry for us, would be content to play. At only 14-18 months she could watch videos all the way through. However, there was no speech. When Em was 16 months old, I asked a dear friend what she thought. Her reply: "Harvey talks for her. She is fine."

If you have received a formal diagnosis for your child's special needs, when did this happen? Do you remember what feelings you experienced at the time and was the diagnosis a hard thing to come to terms with? Have you come to terms with it?

I had my third child, Joel, in November 1999. In January 2000, I took the two of us to a sleep clinic. Emily's Dad had to look after her and Harvey for the day without me. When Joel and I returned home, Carl said to me "There is something seriously wrong with this child. I think she is deaf." I had previously spoken to him about my concerns, but these were rejected—until he had to care for the kids without me.

The first thing we did was call a good friend and speech therapist, Nancy Mills, and go to see her. Within days she had done a report and sent it to our GP and paediatrician. After a few weeks of tests, we were given the diagnosis of classic autism for our Emily. She was 21 months old. I had no idea what this was, and I was told to research it. The specialist told us that, years ago a child like Emily would have been institutionalized, but now early intervention would help. What he could not tell me was how she would progress.

I walked out of the specialist's office with Emily on my hip. A good friend, Josie, had come with me to the appointment—she saw my face and took the keys off me to drive. I felt like I had been given a death sentence for my beautiful girl. She was going to have no life. How did this happen? What is it? What did I—or we—do wrong? Was it our fault? Where does autism come from? I cried and cried.

It was not long after Emily's diagnosis that the place we were living—we had moved from Kununurra to Giru—experienced four floods in one wet season. The floodwater would come under the house, just a slow stream, not a torrent. Harvey and Em would go downstairs with us to see it. Once the two of them went down without us and part of me thought "Well, maybe if Emily drowned that might be the best thing for her as she has no future." I had major depression over Emily's diagnosis and so I sought help immediately. I had to cope with this. I needed to be on antidepressants so that I could be everything to not just Emily, but also Joel and Harvey.

Did you research about how to help your child? What did you do? Which organisations/professionals did you reach out to?

Carl and I researched the hell out of autism. There were many wild and crazy theories circulating about what autism was, where and when it developed in a child, and ways to cure it. My thinking was that I had to do everything I could for Emily so that I could cure it. We got Emily into an early intervention program run in Home Hill in the Burdekin three times a week. We also did weekly speech therapy in Townsville, and the Queensland government had an allied health service that we saw fortnightly. We did so much travelling, it was like Joel, my baby, lived in our car. Ayr did not have a speech therapist. My mother was a councillor in Ingham, so I called her, got the names of politicians, and rang them and lobbied until we got a speech therapist in Ayr.

When Emily was four years old, we were extremely fortunate to be able to see Professor Tony Attwood in Brisbane. He has been her psychologist ever since. There was a speech therapist he recommended, so we saw her too. Classic autism was explained to me as a child retreating into their own world and staying there unless brought out. I learned that you need a team of people working intensively and early on to help a child with autism come out of their world into ours.

One of the hardest things to hear that a therapist ever told me was "We have to get Emily to appear normal." WHAT! My child is *not normal*? Even with a diagnosis and me doing so much learning and running around to speech, early intervention, occupational therapy and so on, I still did not fully accept that Emily had a mental illness. Denial is an amazing thing.

What therapies did/do you use? What routines do you find helpful for your child?

Emily would not look people in the eye. So, it was explained to me that this was something we had to break. We had to get her to look at us in the eye. Doing this with Em's allied health team speech therapist would have me in tears. I was just gently holding Em's face to stay looking forward, forcing her to look into a pair of eyes. Emily would scream and cry as if I were killing her—my heart broke.

HOW DO I DO THIS?

But every session I went to, I stayed and asked questions. I learned all I could. I took on that we had to learn Makaton[29] and Picture Exchange[30]. I learned about over- and under-sensitivity that peeps on the spectrum have and which is a major controller of behaviour. I learned to slow life down and be present. Everything I did had meaning. I followed through with all the work at home. Our house was covered in square white picture tabs so we could communicate with Em.

By six years of age Em started to speak. For some weird reason I thought if I get Em to speak, she will be over this. Denial again…

Everything that came into the house, I cooked from scratch. We would have McDonald's for a treat. Why I thought that was okay I do not know, but Em loved the nuggets and chips and the boys were always with me, driving over 120 km and sometimes 200 km per day to attend sessions.

Em had no sensory issues with foods. Her sensory issues were more about noise. Routine in our family was huge. Our house was a quiet house then—and it still is. We even soundproofed Em's room at one stage. This turned out to be a blessing and made our life so much happier, as the boys could have the TV or something on in the lounge and Em could put up with it. Otherwise it was a matter of dealing with the fighting for control, with Em just coming out of her bedroom to turn the noise off.

---

[29] Makaton is a unique language programme that uses symbols, signs and speech to enable people to communicate. It supports the development of essential communication skills such as attention and listening, comprehension, memory, recall and organisation of language and expression. https://www.makaton.org

[30] Picture Exchange Communication System is a way for people with autism spectrum disorder (ASD) to communicate without relying on speech. To communicate, people use cards with pictures, symbols, words, or photographs that represent tasks, actions or objects. https://pecsaustralia.com/pecs all accessed May 2020

AGE GROUP 20-30

We learned early on to follow through with cause and effect—actions and consequences. Basically, what we teach every child, but with Em it had to be repeated and repeated. Less was more—less words, more impact.

How has having a child with special needs affected your family? Your marriage? Your other children?

I believe Emily's father is undiagnosed Asperger's[31] with bipolar disorder[32]. He cannot cope at all with family life. To this day, he still does not believe that there is much wrong with Em and that I mother her. He hated that the children went to Catholic schools (the private Catholic schools had so much more teacher aide allowance and smaller classes) and would constantly stir up issues for sending them there.

Emily cannot drive a car. Her response time is extremely poor to start with, so much so that going for rides on a push bike was too stressful for me as Emily could not bring herself to stop at a T-intersection on time. So, a car is no option. Her brothers agree with this and say no way. But her Dad still asks when she is getting her licence.

I do not know if Em's disability broke the partnership, but it certainly did not help. Carl was with FIFO (Fly In/Fly Out) but still wanted me to work and look after our young family and house while he went away to his dream job. When he returned, he needed "his" time. So, I was a single mother way before becoming a single mother. I think my eldest Harvey is very Aspie. He has a dual degree in electrical engineering and mathematics. Joel seems to not have the traits as much. I am very tactile. Fabrics are my thing; I love feeling fabrics, and I sew and design. The

---

[31] https://www.healthline.com/health/asperger-syndrome accessed July 2020

[32] https://www.beyondblue.org.au/the-facts/bipolar-disorder accessed July 2020

noise of crinkled paper drives me insane! Tony Attwood said we all have traits but the peeps on the spectrum have them all. There are people with Asperger's on my side of the family and Carl's. I am sure it is genetic.

Harvey and Joel hardly ever had friends around. Our house is normal for us but, it is not everyone else's normal. Emily would walk back from the toilet naked if she had a toilet accident. She needed new clothes and they were in her room. Why put a towel on when you are going to put clothes on? We just never knew when nakedness was going to present. Still to this day it happens. Em might have a towel round her nowadays, but she may also have her butt hanging out the back. But what she sees is covered. The theory of mind. Such an amazing development in humans. Well, in most, but what is so lacking in autism.

How do you take care of yourself? What self-care strategies do you use and how have you been able to implement them?

The care of me comes in the form of a tablet. I live from day to day. I worry about Emily's life without me and if I think too far forward, I fall into a heap. I watch funny movies or binge watch TV to escape. I have a close group of friends that I have always spoken to about every issue in my life.

Do you have a faith? If so, how has this helped you cope with life with your child?

I do not have faith. I lost faith when a close friend lost her two young boys to brain cancer. I believe in science and I believe in the ability of humans to be amazing creatures—good, bad, and indifferent. I was raised a strict Catholic, but besides the calmness I get from reflection and prayers, I do not have faith in a higher being. Collective faith, yes. The power of kindness to heal, the power of laughter to heal, the power of love to shine. I believe man created the stories of a god, as they were not intelligent enough at the time to understand creations and evolution and therefore needed a greater being to justify their existence. But I certainly believe people have the right to believe and not believe, and not be judged either way.

How important/necessary is your family support or the support of your friends/networks? Do you feel as though you have enough support?

My mother was really the only person to help with Emily. When we lived in Ingham or we visited there, Mum would always babysit; having Emily was not an issue. But no one else ever offered. It was all too hard, and I do not think they really wanted to know. Friends would always listen, but they did not help. Maybe I made it look like I was coping just fine.

We are a homebody family. Staying home was less stressful then going out.

What do you hope/think the future holds for your child? Their living arrangements? A job? Marriage and children of their own?

This is very real for me, as I feel as though I am living my words about this right now. Our goals for Em were to enable her to live independently, with support, and be a contributing member of society.

HOW DO I DO THIS?

As I am moving to the United Kingdom and Em is currently refusing to come with us, we have been planning and working towards this goal. But saying that is what we want for Em and then allowing it to happen are two completely different things.

Just recently Emily got sick. I wonder who will look after her when she gets sick and I am no longer here? The support worker will take her to the doctor and so on, but who will stay with her and share love and kindness that is genuine and not paid for? And before that Emily had ringworms and did not know about it. She got very upset with the fact she did not know and realised that one day when I am not here, how will she know she has something if I am not around to help her?

Her legs and bikini line need to be done and hair removed from her face. She put the wrong cream on her face to remove the hair around her lip, chin and side of face and ended up with a large rash in the area that needed medication to help heal. Again, who will help my princess when I am not here? How will she feel when she is not having someone live around her that loves her and cares for her in the way she deserves?

I really hope that Emily looks after her health. When I did not handle the separation from her father, I turned to food, bringing food into the house that I had never brought in before. I used to cook everything we ate, but now there was chips, ice-cream, and chocolate—not alcohol, as I knew I had to be present for my kids (for many, many years I was not *really* present for them). Me having this food meant that Emily also had it. I never taught her to cope with emotions well. Now I am trying to teach Em healthy habits as her health is extremely important, but it is not going so well.

I started two businesses for her, as with the two disabilities combined, it is unlikely that Em will be able to work in traditional jobs. Both businesses have allowed her to learn simple book-keeping and other responsibilities.

The first business was cupcakes. It went well but we really need to move with what people want—making vegan, healthy and savoury treats—and we have not done so. I was trying to earn money and run a business while suffering with depression, so trying to do Em's business as well was just not happening. The support workers were great with the cooking and delivery of cakes with Em, but the business needs social media posts and updating, consistent work and research. I let Em down as I could not do it all, but I hope she will be able to keep it up, as it gives her purpose and worth.

The other business was a paper bin liner and I believe this will be something that can add monetary and social value to Emily's world. It had excellent reach on social media and even got Woolworths' attention. I really want to line the brown paper bin bags with an organic decomposable lining, so the bags can take rubbish that is wet.

I do hope Emily finds a partner so she can have her special person. I want that for her, and I honestly believe there will be that person out there for Em, someone who will be there for her and who she will be there for too. She does not want the sexual side of relationships, but she wants love. However, I do not want her to be taken advantage of. I have taken every precaution to protect Emily from male predators; after I separated from her father, males were not allowed to sleep over when the kids were home. Emily did not go on sleepovers, but she never really had friends who asked her over. I never took respite unless family could have the kids.

What are/have been the joys of raising your child?

I have to say right up front that I never thought I would ever have the mother/daughter relationship that other neurotypical mothers and daughters have, but Em and I have had beautiful moments that I cherish.

Because of Emily, I have become a very patient person. How could I ever get angry or lose my patience with a person who was not deliberately trying to annoy me? The child was only ever trying to survive this world that was so foreign to her. I put my heart and soul into Emily's therapy and she always tried so hard!

It has been a joy seeing Emily, who has so many things going against her and then smashes the expectations, and how she comes alive when something makes her happy. Her reactions are not held back; they are delivered with pure joy.

Emily makes us laugh so much; her funny little sayings and how she sees the world. Her views are mostly innocent. Sometimes she will use a saying she has heard in a film or TV in just the right context and we all stop and laugh that she has been sassy.

What are/have been the challenges of raising your child?

The hardest challenge was coming to terms with the fact that I would never be able to cure Emily's disability. Everything else was just living and it became my life and world—so it was not a challenge, it was life. It was hard trying to make life easier for Em.

The challenge in the family was making sure I gave enough time to my boys. And I guess having depression meant it was a struggle for me to go out and earn a full-time job as Em's father wanted. He blames me for not being able to do this and still raise the family.

AGE GROUP 20-30

What has your child taught you?

Emily has taught me how to live simple and love deeply.

How do you view your child's special needs?

I know the world is made up of many types of people, but I would not wish autism on any family. People with autism look normal but act weird; they are not included; they don't get the world but they could teach all of us in the world so much—that is, there is more to life than material things, Botox, false eyelashes, new cars, sex, skinny beautiful people, duck lips, and new clothes. By helping and caring for people and wanting more for them and others, they can reach the world to be present and pure.

What would you say to other parents of special needs children just beginning their journey? What advice/suggestions would you have for them?

I would suggest to parents starting out on a journey with a child like Emily to give your everything into understanding your child's disability. There are no limits. Get counselling. Have fun and laugh.

If you could think of one word to describe being a parent of a child with special needs what would it be?

Resourceful.

HOW DO I DO THIS?

Any final thoughts?

I have shared my ups and downs of life with a child with autism with my son and his partner, and my other son. I want them to understand the chances of having a child with autism and how it affects relationships. I would not wish autism and intellectual impairment on any person. Life just is not fair or nice to people who are different.

List any organisations in your country that you have found helpful.

- National Disability Insurance Scheme:

- Autism Queensland: https://autismqld.com.au

- Professor Tony Attwood – Minds and Hearts https://mindsandhearts.net/professor-tony-attwood

- Occupational Therapy

- Speech Therapy

- Therapy: Learning to ride a horse: https://www.ranchlands.com.au

TERESA, GRAEME, JOSEPH AND SARAH (AUSTRALIA)

Introduction:

I am Teresa Kent and my husband Graeme and I are both 52; our daughter Sarah is 23 and our son Joseph is 19. Sarah is high functioning autistic with receptive and expressive language disorder[33], Oppositional Defiance Disorder (ODD) [34] and Obsessive-Compulsive Disorder (OCD)[35].

---

[33] https://www.readandspell.com/us/receptive-expressive-language-disorder

[34] https://www.betterhealth.vic.gov.au/health/conditionsandtreatments/oppositional-defiant-disorder-odd

[35] https://www.beyondblue.org.au/the-facts/anxiety/types-of-anxiety/ocd all accessed July 2020

HOW DO I DO THIS?

I have done many different things for a job in my life and when Sarah's disability takes over, I usually end up having to quit whatever employment I am in. This has happened quite a few times, but for the last 11 years I have been employed to support people with special needs and mental health issues, however for many different companies.

My husband and I are also beekeepers, with around 35 beehives[36], and Graeme is also a senior accountant and business consultant[37], so we wear many hats!

We live in Townsville, in Far North Queensland, Australia.

Was it always apparent to you that your child had special needs? If not, when did you notice that something was "different" about your child?

When Sarah was a baby, she was slow in all aspects of her development. I had to go back to work when she was 11 months old and I immediately noticed a difference in my child. This may have been because of all the vaccinations she had to have before she was 12 months old; I do not know. By the time Sarah was 12 months old she would only sleep for 15-minute intervals and would not feed very well. She was late crawling and did not walk by herself (without holding on to anything) until she was 18 months old. Sarah was three years old before she had any speech and when she did speak, it was in one-word sentences. Because she did not have much verbal communication, she would sit on the ground and hit her head on the wall, screaming

---

[36] Aristaeus Honey – Townsville at http://aristaeushoney.buzz

[37] Fairway Group Townsville – Coaching, Taxation, Accounting, Bookkeeping – graeme@fwgs.com.au all accessed July 2020

constantly, testing every single boundary just because she did not get her own way.

If you have received a formal diagnosis for your child's special needs, when did this happen? Do you remember what feelings you experienced at the time and was the diagnosis a hard thing to come to terms with? Have you come to terms with it?

At the age of five, Sarah was diagnosed with ODD. We lived on a farm in country Victoria and, because there was not much funding for special needs, we decided to sell up and move to Canberra, ACT, where there was more funding available (each state has different types of funding). Sarah still only had the ODD diagnosis, but I knew there was more to it; I just did not know what. I did not know what I did not know.

Sarah's diagnosis of high-functioning autism came when she was nine. This only happened because it was suggested we take her to a psychiatrist, who was a specific autism specialist. She asked us to do the WISC[38] test which is basically a Yes/No questionnaire. We had only got to the fifth question before she said, "Your child's autistic". I just cried and cried and cried. For four years we had been under a misdiagnosis, only to find that at the age of nine, Sarah was autistic. Because she is female and high functioning, so she can hold a conversation, it is extremely hard to diagnose. It was just horrific. It was like we—or Sarah—had been living a lie. It was like someone died and we were grieving, and as a family we had to go to counselling.

I have come to terms with it, but my husband has not.

---

[38] https://childpsychologist.com.au/service/assessments/cognitive-assessments-iq-testing/wisc-iv-iq-test/ accessed July 2020

HOW DO I DO THIS?

Did you research about how to help your child? What did you do? Which organisations/professionals did you reach out to?

In those early days again, we did not know what we did not know. We had no idea where to go to get any assistance. We were able to get some real help from our amazing paediatrician, who put us in touch with many Victorian organisations, such as:

- MOIRA Youth, Disability, Family[39] – This organisation helped us with marriage counselling (which is very much needed if you have a special needs kid), with some funding and for Sarah to go on camps. The problem was that most people there had physical and mental disabilities and to Sarah, at her young age, anyone in a wheelchair or who was non-verbal autistic seemed scary to her. In the end, we had to stop sending her because it was the wrong type of help for her.

- Yooralla[40] – This organisation was a huge blessing as they would help with funding for a holiday. When we were at the end of our tether and felt we could not go any further, we would put a price in of, say $700 for a holiday and they would give us at least half.

- SASI (Statewide Autistic Services Incorporated)[41] – In the early stages of help, this was good funding wise. Every year, they would give us an amount of funding which started at $2000 and could go down to as low as $700 over a period of time. I could give them an invoice for $600 for an exercise bike and they

---

[39] https://moira.org.au

[40] https://www.yooralla.com.au

[41] https://www.sasi.org.au

would simply pay it. If the whole family were going to Luna Park, SASI would pay for that. However, their support workers were young and inexperienced, and Sarah ended up being badly injured twice. They did not call an ambulance or even tend to her wounds.

- Presentation Family Centre, Balnarring[42] – These were little units we could put our name down for and use them once a year free of charge. We took our own food, but they also did one big meal for us.

- Bayside Council – We used to get council workers two hours a week from when Sarah was 10 or 11, just so Graeme and I could communicate with each other. The worker would look after the two kids.

What therapies did/do you use? What routines do you find helpful for your child?

Prior to Sarah being diagnosed, we missed out a lot on going out, because she would act out and then we just could not go. If we were going out—for example, if there was a barbeque scheduled for Saturday—we could not tell her, in case it had to be cancelled and she would not understand. For many years, I could not tell Sarah what was going on in advance—and because she did not like change either, this all combined to make things extremely difficult.

---

[42] https://www.presentationfamilycentre.org.au all accessed July 2020

HOW DO I DO THIS?

We had the same routine that we used for *everything*. It went like this:

- Get a drink and a sandwich ready.

- Get dressed.

- Go to wherever we were going—for example, supermarket, doctor, paediatrician, or exercise appointment.

- As soon as we got there, go to the toilet.

- Do the appointment.

- Before we left, go to the toilet again.

- Go home.

For meals, the number three was our magical number that we used. For example, I would cook tacos and put all the ingredients in a big dip platter and the kids had to choose three—such as meat, cheese, and lettuce. Dinner would be meat and three vegetables. If you knew how many times we moved in Sarah's life and how many schools she attended, you would just be blown away with how anyone could do that with an autistic child. Our life the whole time was just chaos.

But what I could control, I did. Which meant the basics every single day with the same routine for getting dressed, for breakfast and so on, as for all the other stuff I had no control over. If Sarah had a meltdown, she had a meltdown. I had no control over this.

In the early days, Sarah did require speech and occupational therapy, she also needed to do exercise otherwise she would pile on the weight because of her medications. At school she was in the soccer team, I bought an exercise bike and different types of exercise equipment to try to get her motivated to do something.

How has having a child with special needs affected your family?

Our family has been deeply affected. In 2012, Sarah was raped in our home. She was 15 at the time and to the police and official people, she was old enough to be home by herself. We thought that she was more intelligent than what she was; and we did not realise the severity of her autism. It was lunchtime, and Graeme and I were both at work. I would ring her to make sure she was okay. On that day, she left the front door ajar to let the cat out. This man came down our driveway just as I was ringing and by the time Sarah got off the phone, he was in the house. Sarah did not say anything that day. The next night she told Joseph and he was only 11 at the time. He went white and then came to me and told me and the whole thing came out.

This was the most horrendous thing that could ever happen to us. If you watch a police drama or one of the murder mysteries, this is exactly what goes on with a crime scene. Detectives put white dust on absolutely everything in our house; I could not touch anything for weeks. They took all Sarah's clothes, bedding, and towels.

The police were in our house when the phone rang. I went screaming "I know it's him!". He had rung the Monday night and he wanted to speak to Sarah and he just kept on ringing. The police organised Graeme to try to organise to meet the man at some place and they finally got him.

We had to go to trial. The Children's Court is hidden—from the outside, no one would know what it is and from the inside it is the most horrible place because the children write words like abuse and rape and draw pictures all over the walls.

HOW DO I DO THIS?

I just cried the whole time. In the law's eyes we were all witnesses, so Joseph was the first witness, I was second and Graeme was third. None of us could hear each other's testimony. Graeme and I had to take the stand and the two kids had to testify via video link to the judge.

Even though she could not see him, the problem was that the perpetrator could see Sarah. She smiled and laughed, so the jury did not believe she was autistic and thought that she was having "a lend" of them. The perpetrator got off, they handed him his passport and he went back to Samoa.

That was the death sentence of our marriage. Graeme turned to drink quite hard and became abusive and just horrible. On my birthday in 2013, my brother-in-law (his brother) said, "I think you better ask him to leave". Our relationship was toxic—we hardly spoke, he slept on the couch and he just did not know how to deal with what had happened. Someone had violated him and his daughter in their own home. No counsellor could erase that. When we would go to counselling it was all for me; they could not help him deal with the s#*t he was going through. We separated after my birthday in 2013, and he took Joseph. This was the worst thing ever, but he had to take him because Joseph, at 12, wanted to bash Sarah's brains in with a crowbar. They moved six hours drive away, to the Victoria/New South Wales border. That was it.

We were in the wilderness for a couple of years and I fought extremely hard to get my husband back. We did not separate for loveless reasons, or because we had found other partners—it was because neither of us could cope with our situation. His coping mechanism was a bad one, and I was not going to condemn him just because he went down that path. I knew he needed help.

AGE GROUP 20-30

How do you take care of yourself? What self-care strategies do you use and how have you been able to implement them?

Early on, I did not take care of myself. I was too naïve and did not understand the full picture. I saw too many specialists and worried too much about where my next meal was coming from. There was no self-care. None.

Whereas now, I am at the stage I can take care of myself because Sarah is 23 and she can sleep for 10, 12 and 14 hours at a time. For me, that is my "absolutely loving it" time—it is pure bliss. You do not wake the sleeping giant if you are not going out!

I take care of myself by talking to the Lord Jesus, which is something I do a lot. I would also take five minutes for myself. I would grab that cup of tea and sit down for a few minutes. But it was hard to do because you are under the pump. You might have two specialist appointments in a day. Everyone is pulling you; the organisations all want a piece of you. It is so hard.

Now that I am through to the other side, I do a lot of self-care by giving myself a face mask or soaking my feet in my foot spa. I book in massages now, where I would never do that early on. I really think I need them at this stage in my life.

Do you have a faith? If so, how has this helped you cope with life with your child?

As a child I was raised Catholic, but I was an atheist in my married life. I had no faith for 12 years and then I started going back to church in 2009 when I came back to Christ. When Graeme and I were early in our separation, I went to Sarah's school, which was a Christian school, and

HOW DO I DO THIS?

spoke to the counselling pastor there. He told me that if you and your husband both stay faithful then there is always a chance of getting back to together. I hung onto that and, with all my heart, I honestly believed that would happen.

Having a faith has certainly helped me cope because at times of stress and distress with my daughter, I look and talk to God. He is always there. Before I came to Christ, I was always screaming "Somebody bloody help me!" and there is no-one there. No-one is going to help you. People do not want to know because it is too complicated; it is just too hard. I was known as "the screaming banshee".

Faith in God is what saved my marriage and faith is what helped me understand my daughter even more so—to have empathy and to grab onto the little sparks of goodness and feel blessed by those things, rather than becoming nasty and narrow minded by hanging onto what Sarah does not do.

Coping by myself without faith for 12 years was hard and the early stages of coming back to the Lord Jesus really helped me. By the time we had gone through Sarah's trial, she had been pretty much out of school for five terms. To the government, she was categorised as a disengaged child and so she could not be put back into a normal school because she had missed too much. Sarah had to go to a school called Oakwood two hours a day, five days a week. The downside of this school was that all of society's wayward children went there. So, there was my autistic daughter, the most normal child out of a bunch of kids who stole, smoked, drank alcohol, and took drugs.

The good thing was that I had been going to church for three years by the time Sarah started at Oakwood. One of the ladies from church suggested we go for coffee at the McDonald's across the road from the school. I knew this lady a little bit, but when we sat down for coffee I basically "verbally diarrhoead" her, telling her everything about this terrible situation I had come upon. To me, I could only see the black. Because she was a woman of faith, she never told me off, never shut me up and never told me not to speak those type of words, and never put me down. I told her one gem (which I did not know was one at the time) and she grabbed onto it, telling me the most amazing things that I could do with this one gem. I cannot even remember this lady's name but that was the turning point for me in my faith journey of understanding Sarah and how to look at things from different eyes. Do not look at our situation from despair, but instead look at our situation from a blessing—and that helped me so much.

I was still cynical, and it takes a long time to change the way you think, and I was simply portraying what had been going on with my life. In my time with Jesus, nothing has ever been instant, but I realised then how terrible I was and how horrible the words coming out of my mouth were. That lady blessed me. I was so horrible—and she blessed me. She taught me a lot.

How important/necessary is your family support or the support of your friends/networks? Do you feel as though you have enough support?

It has only been the four of us (or the two of us, when Graeme and I separated). We have never had enough family support as family members just do not understand our situation. For us as a family unit we have to love—we may not like, but we have to love. Other family members like parents, brother or sister have taken the stance that they do not like Sarah. How do you overcome that? They do not have to visit you, and so they will not. It is a bit tricky if I visit, as I am not allowed to bring Sarah and that makes the situation extremely hard.

HOW DO I DO THIS?

Now we are states away from family and it is difficult for me as I am a nester. All I have ever wanted to do is nest, and in my adult life I have lived in 22 different houses. The only time I have ever nested is when we lived on our farm for nine years.

Family is extremely important when you need a night off as they can look after your child. My Mum passed away in 1997 and my Dad is not trustworthy; I left Sarah with him and I went to pick her up the next morning, only to find he had left her by herself in his house while he went out with his latest girlfriend.

Unless you have a good family, just forget it.

I feel like I have no friends in Townsville and that this is only temporary and not where I am going to die. I have three friends who I have known for 30 years and then the odd one or two friends and acquaintances. In my later life I have ended up with severe anxiety and it is hard for me in Townsville. My life is too emotional and to become attached to other people is also too emotional. You cannot do it, so friends drop off.

What do you hope/think the future holds for your child? Their living arrangements? A job? Marriage and children of their own?

We want Sarah to be moved into supported living accommodation. This would give her a better quality of life because we would not be around and so she would have to get motivated and do stuff for herself. We would be able to have a life; the life we have never had. However, it is a matter of *can* this happen—and I do not know if it will, because of the rape. That is not something that will go away in a hurry; it will be with us for the rest of her life.

AGE GROUP 20-30

Sarah has had part-time jobs before. In Grade 6, her friend's Mum told her "When you are 14 years and 9 months, you come back to my fish and chip shop and I will give you a job". This stayed in Sarah's mind and at 14 years and 9 months she went to the fish and chip shop and said, "Here I am for my job". The boss knew Sarah had a disability in terms of her receptive and expressive language skills, so she could not answer the phone or work the till. Sarah worked every Tuesday night and learned to cook with the hot fats, becoming the best fish and chip cooker and always reliable for extra shifts because she was never out partying. Sarah also worked as a waitress in a Chinese noodle shop in Mallacoota, but it was extremely busy, and she would have accidents.

Here in Townsville she worked for a massage therapist for eight hours a week, which she absolutely loved. Sarah was taught how to wash the towels in the washing machine, put them in the dryer and then fold them in a specific way. She had to clean the kitchen and toilet and the therapy rooms. She had to stop work when Townsville flooded at the beginning of 2019. Now Sarah's health has deteriorated—she has severe gallstones—and she is not able to work.

In the future she probably could work within certain hours. Eight hours a week is good because when it is two four-hour days, allowing Sarah to have breaks. There is a lot of pressure for her to remain focused and on point. She can do the job exactly as her boss wants it done but be like a tightly clenched fist until she gets in the car afterwards and has a meltdown. It was the same for school.

We also taught her how to catch the bus, which took many months. The support worker would follow the bus in the car and made sure Sarah got off at the bus stop. I would pick Sarah up from work, so she did not have to catch the bus home.

Because Sarah cannot look after herself, we do not want her married or with children of her own.

HOW DO I DO THIS?

What are/have been the joys of raising your child?

Sarah has the biggest heart and is the most giving person on the planet and I love her for that. When she was at Oakwood, I was worried for her. I became the school Mum to heaps of kids and there was one girl whose mother and sister were both on drugs and whose brother used to bash her. We went to her house and her bedroom was grey because she did not trust her mother and would not let her mother wash anything. I have never experienced that side of living before and I did not know that type of thing existed. Sarah loved this girl unconditionally and spent five hours cleaning up her bedroom so that she could find her shoes.

During this time, the girl's Dad committed suicide. She had this doona that he had given her. It was grey with dirt, but she would not get rid of it. On Sarah's suggestion, Sarah and I went out and found this big box that we could put that doona in—and then we gifted her a brand-new doona and bedding. This gift came from my church.

Sarah was always the one that waited for the last child, to give that person her last bit of food or her last $5. Even though she is just a bomb sometimes she has the heart of an angel, you know. I am blessed; just really blessed.

What are/have been the hardest challenges raising your child?

Communication. Not being able to communicate and the screaming and not understanding why something is happening.

You can learn as much as you can, but unless you are inside their mind you do not know. The not knowing has been the hardest thing and is where all the challenges come from.

AGE GROUP 20-30

What has your child taught you?

Sarah has taught me how to be an advocate—do not mess with Sarah or you mess with me! She has taught me patience and to take my time. People cannot believe how I act in my life because I am just so calm. Yet 10-12 years ago I was classified as the "screaming banshee".

Sarah has taught me to view the world with a different lens.

How do you view your child's special needs?

I have always told people straight up that Sarah is autistic, and I tell her when she is doing an autistic thing. When Sarah is Sarah and *not* being autistic, she has said to me "Mum, why am I like this? Help me. Why does this happen to me? I don't understand." So for her, she is trapped and it is definitely hard, but I have no problem in telling people Sarah is autistic because if they hear her say something a bit unusual or they see her vague expression they can understand what that means.

Now I know of plenty of families who do not let people know and on the receiving end, it is difficult, because sometimes you cannot determine if that child is naughty or if that child is autistic? To help me overcome people's looks and leers, I simply tell the immediate people around me. For example, when Sarah was young, and we were at the register and she was having a tantrum I would tell people she has ODD. At that stage, that is all I knew. Sometimes, I would lay down and have a tantrum too. People give you really weird looks when you are doing that!

HOW DO I DO THIS?

What would you say to other parents of special needs children just beginning their journey? What advice/suggestions would you have for them?

In the early days, all the information is simply overload. I could not keep up with all the appointments; I did not cope at all and I lost my s#*t so many times!

I would say to parents to try and have time together, just the two of you. That is so important—the Number 1 key to holding it all together. Whether that means an hour after dinner having someone come in and look after your child, or at bedtime, even though you are both exhausted. Try to do something for the two of you. In those early days, it is all about the child and you lose sight of your partner—and if you do not have a partner, you lose sight of yourself.

From 2008, when we lived in Aspendale, Victoria, we had a lady come from the Bayside Council to look after Sarah and Joseph for two hours a week. I remember the first couple of months of having the help, Graeme and I did not even talk because we did not know what to say. We had never been together. For six months we hardly spoke. All we had ever talked about was our horrible situation and our kids and we did not know how to relate to one another.

Ring up a close friend or family member—there has got to be someone there that you can just blah to or cry. I am probably looking at negative aspects here but, in my world, there was nothing positive. To be honest—depending on what the diagnosis was—I do not think there is a rush. One appointment in one day is enough. In one week, it is probably enough! Back then, I tried to "stack em, pack em and rack em" —two and three appointments a day. You are just starting to attempt to come to terms with something that is so wrong, much less listen to what all the professionals are trying to tell you.

AGE GROUP 20-30

Keep it simple.

If you could think of one word to describe being a parent of a child with special needs what would it be?

F#@^%$.

Any final thoughts?

I cannot imagine Sarah not living with us. She has a small package with NDIS which works out at five hours a week, which is not even a support worker's proper full shift. Because Sarah has a mental disability, some days she is good and some days she is not. When we have an NDIS planning meeting, the planners might see Sarah's best two hours of the whole day. They do not see what I see—which is why two NDIS plans have delivered little to really help Sarah.

When I moved from Victoria, the NDIS had not yet happened. Here in Queensland I have only experienced NDIS and no other organisations, simply because when we moved here it was in full swing.

Find help in your immediate community—for example, organisations like Lifeline, Uniting Care, and the Salvation Army. Go to these places and they will give you a long list where you can get help as a family—not necessarily special needs help but assistance with food and clothing. This is a basic thing and I think people need to know that they can get help from these types of community organisations. For example, here in Deeragun, Townsville, there is a place called the Community Hub[43] which is helpful. I take my client there two to three times a week and

---

[43] https://deeragunvillage.com.au/community-hub accessed July 2020

HOW DO I DO THIS?

they get free stuff like bread. These places know how to connect you in. Even if you are in a remote country town, your health service, local Council or the opportunity shops can all be very important ways to start getting connected.

WILLIAM, SANDRA AND NOWELL (AUSTRALIA)

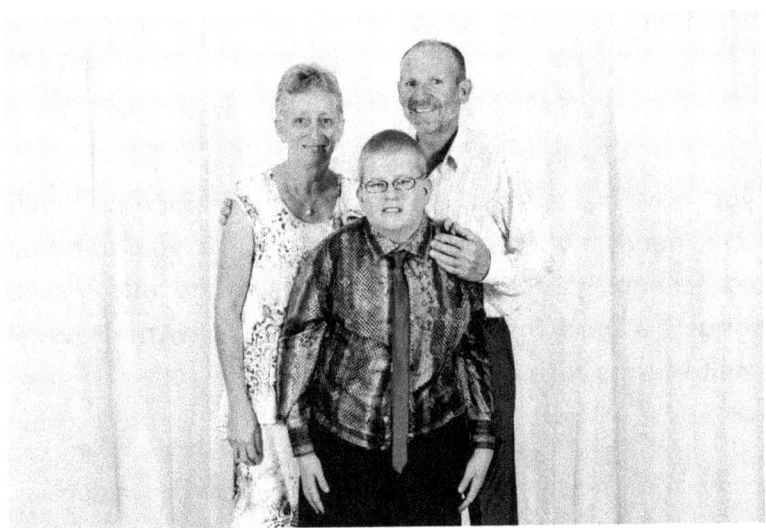

Introduction:

We are the Tento family—William, Sandra, and our adult son Nowell—a family created through the gift of "adoption". Our family began quite differently to what might be considered the norm. In order to start a family, we believe faith and prayer were as necessary as anything else couples do. We are blessed to live in Australia.

HOW DO I DO THIS?

Was it always apparent to you that your child had special needs? If not, when did you notice that something was "different" about your child?

When we adopted our son as a baby, we were aware of his diagnosis and informed (to a certain degree) about the impact this would have on his life.

If you have received a formal diagnosis for your child's special needs, when did this happen? Do you remember what feelings you experienced at the time and was the diagnosis a hard thing to come to terms with? Have you come to terms with it?

Nowell has Prader-Willi Syndrome[44] and, due to being aware of his diagnosis when we adopted him, this was not a hard thing to come to terms with. Consequently, we did not experience grief or loss, but instead we were excited that we were at last starting our family and the possibilities this created.

Whilst we did not experience grief initially, as our son progressed through life—with education, work/employment, social opportunities and living arrangements—there was at times a sense of grief for the aspects of life he would not be able to experience, whilst he worked really hard to achieve the basic goals. However, the reality is that Nowell has achieved many goals above and beyond any expectation we could have had for him. We focus on and celebrate the great gift of the person he is, and the contribution he is making to our family life and our small community.

---

[44] http://www.pws.org.au/prader-willi-syndrome/ accessed July 2020

AGE GROUP 20-30

Did you research about how to help your child? What did you do? Which organisations/professionals did you reach out to?

We researched Prader-Willi Syndrome and tried to link in with professionals who understood this rare genetic condition. We also connected with other families who had children with Prader-Willi Syndrome, which was often difficult to do due to distance. We were also able to network locally with a group of parents who had children with disabilities, and who established a disability service to cater for their needs.

Working with a good paediatrician who was able to link us into appropriate services for Nowell was also invaluable.

What therapies did/do you use? What routines do you find helpful for your child?

An Early Childhood Intervention program saw Nowell having Speech, Occupational, Physio and Psychological Therapies. Speech and Behaviour Therapies continued throughout primary school. Nowell also participated in the local gymnastics club, swimming lessons, piano lessons, swimming club and a Christian children's social club.

A regular routine for daily activities has been critical for stability and success. Despite some professionals advocating exposing children to change, and challenging them to adapt to that, this approach did not quite work for Nowell. Even now, when there is a change to routine, he struggles to cope. When—as is inevitable in life—there are changes due to a series of events, Nowell experiences a meltdown.

How has having a child with special needs affected your family? Your marriage or relationship?

It has been integral for us as a couple to believe in and focus on the same goals, to talk and work together for good outcomes, and to be open to change. Being a parent of a child with a disability encourages you to go back and focus on your marriage commitment. For us, personally, we recall our reasons for making the decision we did and to remember that it was God's plan for our life and if so, God would not abandon us. That being said, we did have some dark days where our focus was not clear, and we drew on each other for encouragement. We also endeavour to have regular prayer time together.

How do you take care of yourself? What self-care strategies do you use and how have you been able to implement them?

We try to celebrate the little things in life as "disability" can often be so constant and such a huge beast that it takes away anything else you would like to have in your life. So, it is critical to "care" for oneself and each other and to respect that each one of us tends to do this in a different way. For example, reading a book, going for a walk, doing craft, visiting a friend and so on.

Do you have a faith? If so, how has this helped you cope with life with your child?

We believe in the Lord Jesus Christ and His promises—we are Christians. Neither William nor I would be the people we are today if we had not said "Yes" to God and adopted Nowell. We are both so much wiser and richer for it.

It was our faith that carried us through our bleak medical experience, when Nowell was critically ill in hospital with a virus in 2019. Family, friends, and our local community supported us through prayer, and I was shown by God a picture of Nowell being carried on a sea of hands reaching upwards. This enabled us to believe God had a plan and was looking after us all.

How important/necessary is your family support or the support of your friends/networks? Do you feel as though you have enough support?

Family have been vital in the early days for support, but as time has passed, often the network is not as strong due to distance and children growing up.

Through an organisation called "Mamre" we did a future planning workshop (various advocacy groups also now present these workshops) and established a "Circle of Support"[45]. We invited a variety of friends with different talents to meet and focus on Nowell's needs and challenges, and plan for the future. Networking with a mix of personalities and experience helped broaden our views and outlook of what opportunities may be available to us. Individuals within the group would then follow up on certain ideas and it was no longer just William and me slogging through things—now the load was shared.

---

[45] https://personcenteredplanning.com/index.php/circles-of-support/ accessed July 2020

HOW DO I DO THIS?

What do you hope/think the future holds for your child? Their living arrangements? A job? Marriage and children of their own?

Currently we are focusing on Nowell moving into independent living and he seems to be looking forward to "doing his own thing".

In our community, Nowell has enjoyed work placement—volunteering at various business houses throughout the week—and this responsibility has boosted his self-esteem.

Life is about living, and we have endeavoured to advocate for and encourage Nowell to "have a go". We hope to expand on this and possibly lead into some regular employment.

What are/have been the joys of raising your child?

Sometimes when we reflect on all the information we were given regarding Nowell's diagnosis, we compare it to having been given a gift with instructions. However just like any gift, there are different models and each range has a different outcome.

So, our son came with a label, but the joys have been in seeing what he can achieve and how much he has accomplished, especially now that he is a young man.

Nowell's greatest gift to us has been his enduring tenacity, resilience, and personality. He has a great sense of adventure and a good sense of humour, he also has faith in God and a deep concept of life.

AGE GROUP 20-30

What are/have been the hardest challenges raising your child?

Constantly having to advocate for our son in all areas of life—education, employment, health, and disability services—has been challenging.

Surgical intervention for scoliosis was one of the major health issues Nowell has dealt with over a period of ten years, involving eight surgeries and resulting in a spinal fusion. This surgery was performed some 1,500 kms away from our home, which isolated us from our family and friends and encouraged us to draw on our faith.

Scoliosis has contributed to a reduction of lung capacity on one side and compromised our son's health. In 2019, Nowell contracted a virus which effectively shut down his lungs and he spent 14 days on life support—for 11 of those days the doctors would give us no assurance that he would survive. Yet despite the grim warnings from medical staff, we strongly advocated for the best life-giving care to be maintained and endeavoured to the best of our ability to see that it was carried out.

As Christians we do GET the message "God has a plan" —an ICU nurse confirmed one night she believed in faith that Nowell was going to survive.

Nowell has now been well for 12 months, but the aftermath of this are struggles with anxiety and the implications of perhaps contracting another virus. Constant reassurance that he is safe and well helps Nowell to cope.

HOW DO I DO THIS?

How do you view your child's special needs?

In the word disability, the prefix "dis" distracts us from "ability". It is important not to let language/labels define who our loved ones are, but to be assured in Christ Jesus that all our needs are met in Him.

What would you say to other parents of special needs children just beginning their journey? What advice/suggestions would you have for them?

- Patience, patience, patience, and perseverance.

- Maintain a healthy relationship with your spouse is critical as your child is relying on you 100%.

- The constancy of caring for a child/adult with a disability is wearing, so develop a plan to have time out, respite and the like.

- Therapies are only as good as the therapist's ability to engage with your child/adult. If this is not working, move on.

- Take one day at a time.

- Celebrate the little milestones—it is only when we can take the little steps that the big steps become achievable.

- It is important to let other people into your life to support you—do not believe you have to do it all yourself—for example, Circle of Support, family, and friends.

- Remember whatever information you have about your child's diagnosis, this does NOT define your child. They are a unique individual and need to be loved ad accepted for who they are.

- Different is good—inclusion is essential.

- Find a good disability support provider.

- We have a family name "Team Tento" and when we say this, it gives us a good opportunity to have a group hug and re-focus.

If you could think of one word to describe being a parent of a child with special needs what would it be?

Growth.

Any final thoughts?

Our goal has always been to encourage Nowell to participate in as much of life as possible—at different times this has been successful, challenging and frustrating—but as a whole, this has allowed Nowell to be exposed to far more of life and grow into the young man he is today.

Please list any organisations in your country that you have found helpful.

- PWSA (Prader-Willi Syndrome Australia) http://www.pws.org.au

- Mamre https://www.mamre.org.au

- Carers support groups https://www.carersqld.com.au

DEBORAH, COLIN, RYAN AND ANDREW (UK)

Introduction:

Hello. Let me introduce you to my family. My name is Deborah, my husband is Colin and we have two boys, Ryan and Andrew. We live in the United Kingdom, just outside of London.

Our story begins in August of 1996 with the birth of our second son Andrew. What a joy! Our family was now complete.

Then, at the age of three our world was shattered when, after a year of being observed by his paediatrician, Andrew was diagnosed with autism.

Was it always apparent to you that your child had special needs? If not, when did you notice that something was "different" about your child?

There were no apparent signs of any type of disability when Andrew was a young baby. After our son's MMR (Measles, Mumps, Rubella Triple Antigen) vaccination at around 18 months, we noticed signs that something was not right. This started with chronic diarrhoea, which progressed with Andrew having up to seven bowel movements a day. There followed loss of words and Andrew would not respond to his name being called. He also began to line objects up into a straight line.

AGE GROUP 20-30

If you have received a formal diagnosis for your child's special needs, when did this happen? Do you remember what feelings you experienced at the time and was the diagnosis a hard thing to come to terms with? Have you come to terms with it?

Andrew was diagnosed around about the age of three. I can recall the day of diagnosis, as though it were only yesterday—it is not a day I will ever forget.

I did not actually feel anything except numbness. My husband and I had little or no knowledge about autism, and we went home and carried on as normal. Sometimes we would catch each other's gaze—at times with words; at others with none. After the numbness had passed, our feelings were of shock. We felt as though we had woken up from what seemed a bad nightmare.

I do not believe we could ever come to terms with the diagnosis; we have just learned to adapt to our son and our lives have been taken over by Andrew's needs.

Did you research about how to help your child? What did you do? Which organisations/professionals did you reach out to?

Research was my calling. After Andrew's autism diagnosis, our very first point of contact was with our wonderful health visitor Gaye. She very gently took us into the traits of autism, and she also guided us into the help and support we could access. Because Andrew had chronic diarrhoea there were also many hospital appointments to attend. We were scared for our son and experiencing exhaustion as we tried to cope with our situation. Our only option at every hospital visit seemed to be medication. This continued for many years and it seemed as though hospital visits took over our lives.

Andrew attended a nursery for special needs and then transferred to a special needs school. Over the year, we were referred to many professionals regarding Andrew's health. At one stage, we thought Andrew may be deaf and we were referred to an audiologist. We were feeling hopeful that our son's hearing could give us the answer to his non-response when we called his name. He had grommets fitted but our hopes were dashed as the consultant informed us that, even if there were a problem with Andrew's hearing, this would not explain the behaviours that he was exhibiting.

I joined an organisation called PACT (Parents of Autistic Children Together) which sadly is no longer available. I also joined a Carers group—Carers of Barking and Dagenham.

What therapies did/do you use? What routines do you find helpful for your child?

Therapies were something that Andrew initially received at school. Later, at the age of 13, he went to a residential school called Prior's Court School, which is based in Berkshire in the UK. This is an independent special school for young people with autism, aged 5 to 20 years, who are all on the autism spectrum and have moderate to severe learning difficulties and complex needs. Prior's Court School works on the same principle as the famous Boston Higashi School (USA)[46] and it

---

[46] www.bostonhigashi.org. Our mission is to help children and young adults with Autism Spectrum Disorder learn to reach their full potential through the methodology of Daily Life Therapy ®. This unique educational philosophy, developed by the late Dr Kiyo Kitahara of Tokyo, Japan, incorporates a broad and balanced curriculum, including academics, art, music, physical education, technology, and social education. Students take on challenges, learn to overcome obstacles, and gain confidence from their own success. Accessed May 2020

was a transformational experience for Andrew. He received Occupational Therapy, Music Therapy and Psychology input. Today, Andrew receives reflexology. We wanted Andrew's education to continue into adulthood and we fought extremely hard for this to happen. Now, at 23, he is still receiving an education and for this we are incredibly grateful.

Routines play a massive part in the life of someone with autism. My son has always had a structured routine from morning until night—for example, if he is going out, he needs to know where he is going. His routine has been able to become less structured as he has gotten older.

How has having a child with special needs affected your family? Your marriage? Your other children?

Now, there is a question!

It has been overwhelming for our family in so many ways. It has been a fight all the way, knocking me to the floor on various occasions but I would always get back up and continue on. I found out a lot about myself; I have great tenacity and guts. Suffice to say, our family has experienced every emotion there is.

Andrew's autism has put a tremendous strain on our marriage. In some ways, it has had a detrimental effect on our older son Ryan—for example, he had to watch Andrew kick me in the stomach when I was changing him and that vision has stayed with my older son. It has also taken away the attention that Ryan needed when he was growing up, but as he has grown into a man, his understanding has made him a loving brother, who has a wonderful heart and a caring nature.

How do you take care of yourself? What self-care strategies do you use and how have you been able to implement them?

Because my thoughts are always with the future of my son with autism and making sure he is getting his needs met, I do not always take care of myself. When I do make time for me, I practice mindful breathing. I also have a passion for music.

Do you have a faith? If so, how has this helped you cope with life with your child?

In times of need, we tend to turn to God, and I have prayed many times.

How important/necessary is your family support or the support of your friends/networks? Do you feel as though you have enough support?

Family support is key, and we got through this together *because* we are together.

We do not have many friends because of the nature of Andrew's disability.

My extended family are very supportive, but they have their own lives to live.

I do not think you can ever have enough support when dealing with a disability.

AGE GROUP 20-30

What do you hope/think the future holds for your child? Their living arrangements? A job? Marriage and children of their own?

My hope for my son's future is for him to gain more independence. Andrew will always need 24-hour care, because if left to his own devices he would not be able to do anything. He needs to be prompted for much of his day and he is where he needs to be. Why change something that is working?

With support, I am sure there are some things he could do. Presently, Andrew is doing some gardening, helping in an allotment for the Wilderness Foundation[47], as part of his education, and he has helped in The Marven Stables[48].

Because of the nature of his disability, Andrew will never marry and have children. He lacks the mental capacity to make decisions pertaining to his life.

What are/have been the joys of raising your child?

It has been wonderful to watch Andrew mature and to see his character develop.

Communication has been our goal for Andrew, as he lost the three words that he did have after his MMR vaccination at 18 months of age. To see him communicate with an IGrid Communication Tool—where

---

[47] The Wilderness Foundation – Essex at https://wildernessfoundation.org.uk/venues/essex, located in Melbourne, Chelmsford, Essex.

[48] The Marven Stables, www.myequinelife.co.uk/business/marven-stables all accessed May 2020

he can put in a word or sentence and the IGrid speaks the word or sentence back—has been a great joy.

Another joy has been watching Andrew now being able to eat many different foods, as his diet used to be very bland when he was a little boy—seeing him eat a banana was a huge moment! It has also been a big relief to see a reduction in the constipation medication he has been on for most of his life.

What are/have been the hardest challenges raising your child?

In all honesty, the hardest challenge has been accepting Andrew's disability, which as I said earlier, I do not think is possible; rather, we just learn to manage the disability.

It really is a challenge every day with our son. We never stop learning about Andrew's disability and getting others to understand about our son's special needs has been difficult. It has been an ongoing fight to secure what Andrew needs and we have had to educate various agencies, because all they see is what it is all going to cost. But by educating ourselves, we have become well equipped with the knowledge of how to fight for what is needed for Andrew.

What has your child taught you?

My child has taught me that I had no idea I had so much love for this vulnerable boy—and that love has grown to excess. Andrew has taught me patience. He has taught me about autism!

Tenacity was already in my genes, but he has helped that to grow. My son has taught me to fight for him and to advocate for him.

AGE GROUP 20-30

How do you view your child's special needs?

My son's disability is something that makes him special. I see it as my work. God does not want me to rest on my laurels and I believe He gave Andrew to me because He knew that I could handle the journey. God did not see that there would be a few blips on the way—or maybe He did, and He put them there to see how I would handle it! I fell once (that is a story for another time) and now I am back, a little more fragile; but when I am fighting, I seem to find the strength from somewhere.

What would you say to other parents of special needs children just beginning their journey? What advice/suggestions would you have for them?

Advice that I have for other parents is to allow yourself to feel whatever it is you feel. Do not put pressure on yourself; you will find your own way of dealing with this disability. You are not perfect—there is no such thing.

Give yourself time to breathe and take each day as it comes. Every emotion is coming your way, but you will learn so much! Your child is special, and they have the best parent that they can have because you will learn to fight for everything they need.

You do not know how remarkable you are, but you will find this out as you go forward in this journey.

If you could think of one word to describe being a parent of a child with special needs what would it be?

Resilient.

HOW DO I DO THIS?

Any final thoughts?

This is just a very, very small snippet of our journey. It has been a real pleasure to have been able to share just a small piece of our journey with Meredith for this book. Our journey is a lifelong one; it will never finish but we keep educating and fighting for our son.

Please list any organisations in your country, or other resources, that you have found helpful.

Organisations:

- Prior's Court School: https://www.priorscourt.org.uk

- Carers of Barking and Dagenham www.carerscentre.org.uk

- The Wilderness Foundation – Melbourne, Chelmsford, Essex https://wildernessfoundation.org.uk/venues/essex

- The Marven Stables www.myequinelife.co.uk/business/marven-stables

Resources:

IGrid Communication Tool, www.thinksmartbox.com

AGE GROUP 20-30

Books:

- *"Silenced Witnesses, Volume 1 – The Parents' Story: The Denial of Vaccine Damage by Government, Corporations and the Media"* (2008), Edited by Martin J. Walker, CryShame with Slingshot Publications London.

    Available at orders@sensinetbooks.com

- *"Silenced Witnesses, Volume 2 – The Parents' Story: The Denial of Vaccine Damage by Government, Corporations and the Media"*, Edited by Martin J. Walker, Slingshot Publications London 2009.

    Available at orders@sensinetbooks.com

GABRIELLA AND JORDAN (AUSTRALIA)

Introduction:

Hi, I'm Gabriella. I have been a single mother to my son Jordan since he was ten years old, when his father died suddenly from a heart condition. Jordan is now 24 and has Fragile X[49], autism, and intellectual impairment.

We live in North Queensland.

Was it always apparent to you that your child had special needs? If not, when did you notice that something was "different" about your child?

My son was born by caesarean section and he was a beautiful healthy boy, weighing in at 9 lbs. There were no problems. He breastfed and was developing well until the age of 18 months, when he had his MMR vaccination. Shortly afterwards, Jordan began to show unusual symptoms—he lost whatever speech he had; he would not look at us and avoided eye contact. He was just not himself. It was like we had lost our little boy and someone else had replaced him.

This was the start of a long and harrowing journey.

---

[49]https://www.fragilex.org.au/understanding-fragile-x/ accessed July 2020

AGE GROUP 20-30

If you have received a formal diagnosis for your child's special needs, when did this happen? Do you remember what feelings you experienced at the time and was the diagnosis a hard thing to come to terms with? Have you come to terms with it?

Our GP diagnosed autism and so off we went to a paediatrician. After many visits and blood tests, Jordan was also diagnosed with Fragile X Syndrome, an inherited condition with a fault on one of the chromosomes. My partner and I felt absolutely devastated and shellshocked. We had so much to get our heads around—life as we knew it would never be the same again. I fell into a state of depression, but I had to keep going for the sake of our little boy.

I cannot believe it has taken so long, but it has only been in the last 12 months that I have accepted and adjusted to Jordan's diagnosis.

Did you research about how to help your child? What did you do? Which organisations/professionals did you reach out to?

As parents, the situation we found ourselves in led us to automatically go into research mode. We joined the Fragile X Association and autism support group in our local area and tried to get as much information as we could. We attended everything we could—workshops, autism conferences and many meetings.

When it came time for Jordan to start school, we had a choice for him of inclusion at a regular school or attending a special education and development unit. Our preference was for regular school, but because Jordan would run away a lot, it was decided he needed the more secure environment of the special school. Initially, we were incredibly sad about this, but it turned out well, as the school was marvellous and did their best for my son. Jordan was getting support and we were learning new ways to interact and play with him. The guidance officer tested him and as a result, intellectual impairment was added to his diagnosis.

What therapies did/do you use? What routines do you find helpful for your child?

We were able to access speech and occupational therapy for Jordan, starting when he commenced kindergarten and then school.

He loved going to school because he had a fixed routine mapped out for him and it worked well. Routine still works well for Jordan; he works with visual pictures and preparation for outings—knowing where he is going and what he is going to be doing each day. Once he knows this, he is calmer, and things run much smoother.

How has having a child with special needs affected your family?

Sadly, my family was torn apart when my partner died suddenly. This was the saddest part of my life and I was absolutely devastated by the loss. I had been coping reasonably well with the two of us looking after Jordan. The stress involved with having a child with special needs puts a lot of pressure on your relationship and you must both be on the same page with regards to making decisions for your child's upbringing.

When I became a single mother, I tried to manage as best I could, but I was shellshocked, to say the least. I had to learn to accept help, which was a big one for me. It is amazing what you can do when faced with adversity.

With my family (and friends), I have tried to educate them on how to react to and treat my son. Once they knew about his disability, it helped so much. They were then able to educate their children to accept and include him as much as possible.

How do you take care of yourself? What self-care strategies do you use and how have you been able to implement them?

A bit of retail therapy goes down well. I love hairdressing appointments, a glass of wine and brie on crackers, manicures and pedicures for relaxation, regular meetings with my girlfriends for coffee, going to the movies and massages, which help me wind down and de-stress. I walk every night for 45 minutes with my neighbour, which I think is hugely important for my mind and body, and for venting feelings.

My depression comes and goes but is controlled well with anti-depressants and having a group of supportive friends to meet up with for coffee and chats to unwind, swap stories and chill out and have a laugh. This is extremely important to me.

To regain my sanity, I also make sure Jordan goes to a respite house on a Friday and Saturday night every six weeks.

Over time, I have learned to switch off and know my limitations, so I do not end up a weeping mess.

Do you have a faith? If so, how has this helped you cope with life with your child?

I was brought up a Catholic by my parents. I have my own personal connection with God and faith in Him to help me through the bad times and to share the good times with. Even though I no longer attend church, I am happy with this special arrangement.

How important/necessary is your family support or the support of your friends/networks? Do you feel as though you have enough support?

Support means everything to me. I believe that we must seek support from family, friends, and networks. I have fought hard—and I am still fighting—for my son to have the support he needs. Jordan deserves the best support possible and I feel I am getting this now through NDIS, but I still must negotiate and co-ordinate everything. There is never a dull moment.

What do you hope/think the future holds for your child? Their living arrangements? A job? Marriage and children of their own?

I would like my son to live independently, with 24-hour support, in his own home. I know this is possible, but for this to happen, his support must be on track. I need caring and loyal workers who genuinely like to spend time with my son and help him to live a fulfilling life.

Jordan is happy with the simple things in life—a routine and balanced day with good rest and good meals; and for him to be loved and cared for and to feel safe and secure with his support team. This is especially important for me.

I would dearly love him to have a paid or volunteer job for a couple of hours a day that he enjoyed going to. I am sure that Jordan would feel proud and useful to be part of a team. He could pack things, and he likes filling drink machines up. He has not reached his full potential and there is plenty more that he can do, with support, but so far nobody has done anything like that with him.

Jordan has a special vest that the tradies wear, and he loves its neon fluorescent colours. He puts this vest on and pretends to be a tradie. He also likes company uniforms and recognises their emblems, like the one for the Commonwealth Bank.

I think my son would like a girlfriend as a mutual caring friend and companion.

What are/have been the joys of raising your child?

Watching Jordan grow in body and mind and shaping him into a kind and loving sort of person—which he has turned out to be—has been a joy. He is a nice person who can fit into the community. I feel enormously proud of what I have done. We are both learning about each other as we grow. He knows who he likes and who he dislikes.

He loves his Mum.

It is amazing what comes out of Jordan's mind. He points at pictures of things he would like to do. He loves going shopping and to parades and he wants to go to Movie World to see Superman. Jordan also has a great sense of humour and he surprises me with his antics.

What are/have been the hardest challenges raising your child?

The hardest challenge is to keep myself mentally and physically well, so that I can look after my son. It has been so hard to deal with not having any family around, due to distance. I have envied people who had close family nearby and wished things could have been different.

Life as a single Mum is so particularly challenging when it comes to making decisions about every aspect of Jordan's life. I question myself "Did I make the right choices for my son?" Gaining support and funding for therapies for Jordan has also been a huge challenge. You could write a book on this alone!

It was also a massive challenge dealing with Jordan when he gets angry. As he grew up, his hormones kicked in and he could get aggressive. It was just so full on for me trying to keep everything together. We had to see the GP and the psychiatrist about his aggression, and Jordan was put on a dose of Risperidone[50]. He is so much calmer now, but he can—depending on the situation—still show anger. It is hard to explain, but I did not realise how my son felt about things. Sometimes he just wants to be left alone. He gets sick of being told what to do; of me, of people and going out and he just likes to be in his room. I guess this is his way of chilling out. Working with his visual pictures and being prepared for outings calms him and helps things run much more smoothly.

What has your child taught you?

Jordan has taught me love and perseverance, forgiveness, patience and how to be an advocate (I did an advocacy course). Because he has accepted himself, he has taught me acceptance of the conditions we live under. Once I could do this, I was much happier within myself. I did not think I had to fix him, but I wanted him to be like other people without special needs. I have realised this is not possible and that my

---

[50] Risperidone, or Risperdal, is an antipsychotic medicine that works by changing the effects of chemicals in the brain and is used to treat schizophrenia and symptoms of bipolar disorder.

expectations were much too unrealistic. Jordan is a lovely person as he is, and all that matters is that he is happy and well-adjusted.

I was always fighting. Fighting to get Jordan talking, fighting for him to eat healthy foods (he would only eat junk food), and to wear other clothes besides the stretchy ones he likes. I have come to accept that Jordan is his own person and now we live much happier.

I find it hard to believe it took so long for me to accept Jordan as he is, and that he needs a lot of help and to just get stuck into it. It has also taken the longest time for me to not feel guilty about Jordan's diagnosis. It is a bit like learning technology—you can only do so much with the circumstances you are given. Once I accepted Jordan as he is—while still doing the best I can for him—I felt the pressure lift.

Jordan has also taught me how to be strong and to face up to people who are wrong. I used to be a people pleaser, but I no longer take this.

How do you view your child's special needs?

Disability makes my child unique and needs to be embraced. Jordan is a quiet achiever who is capable of so much; there is so much more to him that needs to be discovered and explored.

What would you say to other parents of special needs children just beginning their journey? What advice/suggestions would you have for them?

Learn to be patient with your child. They take extra time to express their needs. I used to be very impatient to do stuff with Jordan. I had to sit back and allow double the time for him to do things. This was hard to get used to, but something I needed to learn.

HOW DO I DO THIS?

No matter how strong and independent you think you are, learn to accept help. This is a big one! If at first you are unable to access good help, keep trying, as there is always someone out there. Have backup numbers that you can ring depending on the situation.

Treat yourself gently. Get outdoors and into nature with your child. Be calm; they will pick up on your stress and it does not help anybody if you are stressed.

You must get a good support group around you; it is a rough road you will be travelling.

Have time out if you can—just to recharge and get back on track.

If you could think of one word to describe being a parent of a child with special needs what would it be?

I had to have two words—challenging but rewarding. There are so many challenges but so many rewards.

Any final thoughts?

I found answering these questions to be therapeutic. I do not always think of all the good things about my son, and it has been good to write down things to sort them out in my head and to realistically show me where Jordan and I are at.

Things have changed a lot since the early days with my son. Things are much easier now, with organisations like AEIOU and with the NDIS funding.

There is always hope!

AGE GROUP 20-30

Please list any organisations in your country that you have found helpful.

- Carer Gateway Support Services (Wellways) at https://www.wellways.org/carers. This has replaced Carers Queensland. This is a national support service funded by the Australian Government, providing free support through a network of regional Carer Gateway Service Providers.

- Friends Care Online is our own Carers Facebook group by Carers Queensland, where we keep in touch with fellow carers. We organise meet ups like going to the park and going out for coffee and lunches.

    I never found that mothers group thing helpful, but I find this group is good.

- For respite, Commonwealth Carelink is available. Go to: https://www.dss.gov.au/...commonwealth-respite-and-carelink-centres.

- AEIOU is an NDIS-approved service provider for autism-specific early intervention. Their website is https://aeiou.org.au and you can attend a free information session where you will receive up-to-date, relevant information, or talk directly to their NDIS Support Co-Ordinator.

MEREDITH AND SARAH (AUSTRALIA)

Introduction:

My name is Meredith and I am a Mum to two daughters—my younger girl is 22 and my elder is Sarah, who is 25. I also have three stepdaughters, two of whom have children of their own, so I am very blessed.

My Sarah is non-verbal autistic, with sensory processing disorder[51], epilepsy and—due to our difficult family life when she was growing up—suspected post-traumatic stress disorder. We live in Townsville, Queensland, Australia.

---

[51] https://spdaustralia.com.au/ accessed July 2020

AGE GROUP 20-30

Was it always apparent to you that your child had special needs? If not, when did you notice that something was "different" about your child?

Sarah was born in foetal distress by emergency caesarean; she was inhaling the meconium (the waste matter) and this was life-threatening; they had to get her out quickly. She was in a humidicrib for the first couple of days, but I was still able to breastfeed her. All seemed well.

For the first few weeks of Sarah's life, despite having bad colic, she was thriving and hitting her milestones. Then Sarah's father had a dispute with our landlord, and we had to leave our home and live on our business premises (we had a therapeutic massage and alternative healing practice). This was a very unsettling time and I am certain this transferred to Sarah. By about six weeks of age I was worried that Sarah was having trouble making eye contact with me, and I took her to see an experienced paediatric nurse. The nurse assured me all was well, but I just could not shake the feeling that there was something very wrong. Shortly after this, I attended a new mothers group and it was obvious to me that Sarah was not like other babies of her age. She looked quite sickly and would not engage much with other people or her surroundings.

From when she first went on to solids, at four months of age, Sarah suffered from severe constipation. I would have to give her small suppositories and this would be so distressing for her. I felt like I was violating her, but it had to be done as she was so blocked up. She seemed floppy and used to arch herself backwards and I remember she only rolled over once. From about six months, one of her eyes had started to turn. At nine months, she still could not sit up properly. By the age of 12 months, Sarah was given various tests at the Royal Children's Hospital in Melbourne, but nothing was found to be amiss. I was told that all babies develop at their own pace and to come back again if I continued to be worried.

Sarah had developed some speech, but by the time she had her MMR (Measles, Mumps, Rubella) vaccination at 18 months of age, this was completely gone. I do believe her vaccinations were too much for her system. From the research I have done, I believe it would have been wiser to get the vaccines done singly, not three at a time as in the MMR, and to space them further apart. I believe her failure to thrive and the stress in her young life meant her immune system was far too fragile for her to cope with so many vaccinations in such a short space of time.

By the time Sarah was two and a half there was no denying there was something seriously wrong. She was not yet walking, even though she had been crawling for over a year. When she crawled, she would drag one of her legs. Sarah was nowhere near toilet trained, she had no speech and, apart from pointing at things, there was little engagement with people or her surroundings.

If you have received a formal diagnosis for your child's special needs, when did this happen? Do you remember what feelings you experienced at the time and was the diagnosis a hard thing to come to terms with? Have you come to terms with it?

Sarah's first diagnosis was severe intellectual impairment, when she was around three years of age. There were three or four different specialists doing tests and asking me questions and I remember feeling disconnected from the whole process. I felt like a hopeless mother, but I was also relieved to get the professional recognition that my daughter's development was not normal and now she could finally get some help.

Sarah was able to access early intervention two mornings a week. She was in a small group of five children and I was able to stay with her. I learned so much from the amazing staff who worked there; everything was done through play and Sarah made so much progress.

When Sarah was five, we moved to Tasmania and she was eligible for a one-on-one teacher's aide in a mainstream Prep class. In those days, autism was quite rare, especially for girls, and in Tasmania diagnosis for autism was not best practice until a child was at least eight years of age. Sarah's teacher aide, her teacher and I all suspected for at least two years that Sarah was autistic and finally, at eight, she was given the formal diagnosis by a psychologist. Even though I suspected it, it was still incredibly hard to hear those words that made autism a reality for my girl. I remember feeling grief stricken and devastated, but also that I had to hold things together in front of the psychologist. I would not allow myself to experience the full extent of my feelings at that time, as I am sure I would have collapsed into depression and then be unable to properly care for my daughters. I knew there was a long and challenging road ahead of us.

Sarah being autistic has been a hard thing to come to terms with and for many years I believed autism was a medical disease that Sarah *had*, and that I was convinced I could cure. I tried to "fix" Sarah's condition and I believed she could recover and become "normal", given the right treatments and interventions.

I have now come to terms with the precious value and uniqueness of my daughter, but at times I do feel sadness that she needs so much support. I strive to ensure my daughter has the best care and support possible, and that she is given every opportunity to reach her full potential.

HOW DO I DO THIS?

Did you research about how to help your child? What did you do? Which organisations/professionals did you reach out to?

When Sarah was three years old and we were attending the early intervention class, I made friends with two other mothers who both had autistic children. Each of us noticed our children were severely constipated and that their general health had gone downhill after the 18-month MMR vaccination. I wondered if there was some connection with our children's behavioural challenges and them being so constipated. That begin a journey of research as I uncovered the connection between gut health and the brain. I was in research mode for many years. I wore myself out, literally, reading so many books and doing so much research, mostly over the internet but also through attending conferences and courses.

The nutritional aspect really captured my interest and around the time Sarah was five I put our whole family on Dr Sandra Cabot's liver cleansing diet. Sarah's constipation eased and we all benefited health wise. Then when Sarah was thirteen, I removed gluten and dairy from her diet. She had been punching holes in the walls and the change in diet helped her moods, and she was much happier in herself. I also made sure she had minimal processed and sugar foods.

At the beginning of our marriage, Sarah's father and I had a therapeutic massage business and over the years I tried many different alternative therapies to help Sarah: kinesiology, homeopathies, naturopathy, Bowen therapy, different nutritional nasal sprays, DNA testing, a candida cleanse and testing for Pyrrole disorder[52], which came back positive and required zinc supplements. Getting Sarah's gut right has been an ongoing challenge and for much of her life she has been bloated. I have

---

[52] https://www.brisbanelivewellclinic.com.au/pyrrole-disorder/

recently consulted a dietician who assures me we can resolve the bloating. Sarah has also gained a lot of weight from being on Risperidone, which the dietician says is because the medication has caused a spike in her body's insulin production. A diabetic diet has now been prescribed.

Sarah over the years had occupational therapy. When she was three and four years of age, she had outreach occupational therapy and two wonderful therapists would come to our house and do a session with her every week which was immensely helpful. We also had speech therapy over the years, mostly when Sarah was younger, but it tapered off during her high school years. Now Sarah is making excellent progress as an adult with a fantastic speech therapist.

When she was 17, I read a book about neuroplasticity of the brain called *"The Brain That Changes Itself"* and there was a recommendation for a program called Fast ForWord[53] to help with speech. Sarah would do the online exercises—they were structured like games—for a couple of months and then she would stop. It was like she would get filled up and then it was too much to cope with. We stopped and started this program quite a few times.

Through our disability services provider, I also secured funding for an individual mentorship program for Sarah with Tali Field-Berman, a world-class autism specialist, and this helped enormously with Sarah's many challenges.

Over the years I have kept all the paperwork for every test, every IEP and school report in a big folder. This helps me to see the journey my daughter has taken, and I am in awe at what she has gone through and accomplished.

---

[53] https://soniclearning.com.au/ all accessed July 2020

HOW DO I DO THIS?

What therapies did/do you use? What routines do you find helpful for your child?

I have covered a lot of the therapies we used but it was hard to do anything consistently because we moved around so much in the early years of Sarah's life. I was a single parent even when my husband was present and so I never had a lot of support to bring Sarah "into the real world" as it was just too hard for one person to cope with all Sarah's challenging behaviours and be in a domestic violence situation. I was often in damage control and on survival level.

Things were more settled by the time Sarah was of school age and she had a one-on-one teacher's aide in a mainstream class at her first primary school in Tasmania, which she attended until Year 5. We moved to Queensland and Sarah was able to complete her schooling in the same town.

Visuals were extremely helpful. Sarah had a visual timetable at school and at home, so she would know when things were happening. She got particularly good at PECs (picture exchange communication[54]) when she was eight years old and the teachers consistently used it in her primary school years. She still uses pictures as one of her ways to communicate. Sarah had a lot of intervention around toilet training and for two years she would go to the toilet at timed intervals until she was trained. It was a wonderful day when she no longer needed nappies! Sarah refused to wear nappies at night at around that time, and she stayed dry from then on, only ever having an accident if she was unwell.

She also did Horseriding for the Disabled but stopped this because she would travel for 75 minutes to be on a horse for 10 minutes and this, understandably, was very frustrating for her and so Sarah would act out on the drive home. She also loved swimming and she learned to swim

---

[54] https://pecsaustralia.com/pecs/ accessed July 2020

well; her Tasmanian primary school built this into part of her program and her aide took her weekly. This was wonderful for Sarah.

I always had the same bedtime routine for my girls when they were little. I always tucked them in and read bedtimes stories to them. This was like a reset, a way of saying that, no matter what had gone on in the day, all was right with the world. I also made sure I cooked with them. Sarah never had any sensory issues with food, so this was a lovely way to spend time together.

How has having a child with special needs affected your family? Your marriage? Your other children?

It has greatly affected our family. It was like we were the walking wounded—always on high alert and barely surviving. I wonder sometimes how things could have been for Sarah had her father been more of a stable force in our marriage. Sarah's father and I separated once and for all when she was 15 and then later divorced. I believe the domestic violence Sarah witnessed had a huge impact on her and contributed to her challenging behaviours.

For many years, after her father and I separated, Sarah exhibited the violent behaviours of her father towards me and her sister. She was also self-harming. As a young child, Sarah used to bite the back of her hand and hit her head and as she grew older, she would pick and tear at her lips, wrists, legs, and toenails. Seeing my child hurting herself was extremely hard and it was almost impossible for me to manage this behaviour.

My younger daughter's needs were usually secondary to Sarah's and so to try to make up for this, I would spend one-on-one time with her, doing things like going out for breakfast or shopping. I would make sure Sarah was cared for when there were school events for her sister, but as a family we did not go to places like markets, family fun days, sporting activities or holidays like ordinary families did. We could go to big outdoor spaces such as the park and the beach and to things organised and supported by our disability support organisation such as bowling, swimming, the movies and to an indoor playground called Kids Paradise in Launceston, Tasmania.

How do you take care of yourself? What self-care strategies do you use and how have you been able to implement them?

When Sarah was younger, I rarely did any self-care. Sometimes the disability support organisation we were part of in Tasmania would organise pampering days for the Mums and this was lovely. I would get an occasional massage. From when Sarah was 11, I started to access respite, and have a break that way.

As Sarah grew older, I accessed as much respite as possible. But this was often never enough, especially when Sarah was very violent. Tali, my online mentor, gave me some good self-care strategies, including finding a creative outlet. At the time, I used to paint patterns with watercolours. For exercise, I did some Bootcamps and walked regularly. I would make sure to connect with other mothers through a Facebook group I set up called Autism Mums and I also made friends with other Mums in real life, meeting for coffee and lunch and occasional weekends away. In my experience, other mothers who have children with special needs can offer understanding and support in such a deep and uncomplicated way, and this is truly priceless.

After I got divorced, I felt a lot freer to take care of myself and I get regular massages. My faith in God and relationship with Jesus is my ultimate self-care and a whole new world has opened up to me now. I love to read my Bible and prayer is my lifeline to God.

I have also been able to develop my love of writing. Over the years, I would journal on and off as a way of processing what was happening with Sarah. There was a time when Sarah became dangerously ill with an undiagnosed sickness which had originated from a urinary tract infection. Through a chain of events which I can only describe as miraculous, I ended up writing my first book[55] about this time in my life. When I was feeling desperately alone and fearful as to what might happen with Sarah, I recorded the words of comfort and help that the Lord Jesus spoke to me about. Writing is my creative outlet now and the book you are reading is my fourth one—each of these covers an aspect of my life.

Do you have a faith? If so, how has this helped you cope with life with your child?

I used to be in the New Age before Sarah was born; and I believed in a universal higher power. I considered myself to be spiritual, leaning towards Buddhist philosophy. It did not enter my head that I would ever want to be a Christian. I thought it would be a stifling, boring thing to be one of those judgmental Christians. But, as my life unfolded and I experienced the crippling entrapment of being in a domestic violence situation, as well as having a child with special needs, New Age teachings no longer gave me any sort of comfort.

When I heard the good news gospel message about how Jesus sacrificed his life for me—as the way for me to get right with God—and then overcame that death by rising from the grave after three days, it really

---

[55] http://www.amazon.com/dp/B075HHRNPG

HOW DO I DO THIS?

spoke to my heart. I willingly repented and turned from all I had done in my old life. I accepted the gift of grace and forgiveness from Jesus, taking a leap of faith to give my life to him. I had a born-again experience and I became a new creation, which was like going from a life of black-and-white to one in full technicolour. This was a miraculous and supernatural event not easily explained to someone who does not know Jesus—and something that must be experienced to be believed.

The gift of salvation is available for everyone and each person must freely choose whether they want to be separated from God or to be reconciled to Him through His son Jesus. As the Holy Bible says in *John 3:16 For God so loved the world that He gave His one and only Son, that whoever believes in Him shall not perish but have eternal life. 17 For God did not send His Son into the world to condemn the world, but to save the world through Him.*

Everything began to change for me, especially regarding the worries I would have as far as Sarah is concerned. I can give all my worries to Jesus, and I can rest easy that she is in good hands with Him. One of my favourite scriptures is *2 Timothy 1:7 For God has not given us the spirit of fear; but of power, and of love, and of a sound mind.* He has assured me "As much as you love her, I love her more. I have a plan for her life" —and I believe this with all my heart. I have relaxed a lot and can lean on Jesus through good and bad times. Prayer and being part of a church family has been invaluable to help me cope. I am very much an introvert and used to find it hard to reach out to people, but walking with Jesus means I now realise it is okay to ask for help and it is okay to let people know who I am; that I do not have everything together and that I cannot do everything.

I am nowhere near as exhausted because I can give my burdens to Him. I am never alone. The Bible teaches me what I need to know to make sense of this life and it also explains everything that is currently going on in this world that we live in (for example, the COVID-19 pandemic that we are experiencing at the time of writing this book). Because of Jesus, my life has been transformed. It is not because of anything I have had to do, but rather it is all because of what He did for me—and you—2000 years ago on that cross.

How important/necessary is your family support or the support of your friends/networks? Do you feel as though you have enough support?

Support has always been very necessary, but it was not always easy for me to accept just how important it was and how much we needed it. Sarah's stepsisters have always loved and wanted to know Sarah, but they have not always been able to be in her life due to distance. It was the same with my family. My parents lived in another state and we got to holiday with them every now and then. When Sarah was eight, we stayed with my Mum for her eightieth birthday and Sarah patted Mum's face and said "Grandma" clearly. This was an incredibly special moment because Sarah had not spoken a word for many years. My Mum adored Sarah. My Dad was also very patient and caring with her.

My elder sister and her family are all very accepting of Sarah, and it is lovely to spend time with them—again, we live a long way from each other and so the family support has been hard to get because of the physical distance. Sarah's father's parents were not supportive at all and had little to do with her as they did not understand her special needs—nor did they want to. My other daughter is also a great support. Her relationship with Sarah has been fragile due to the violence that has been inflicted on her by her sister, but I know she loves her and is there for her. I do feel as though I have great support from friends and the support organisations that work with Sarah.

HOW DO I DO THIS?

My faith in God and my relationship with Jesus provides me with enormous support. Every life situation is addressed in the Bible and I can rest in the promises of God and know that He is faithful and good. At the end of the day, Jesus is constant on this hard journey and I want to do the best I can for both my daughters.

What do you hope/think the future holds for your child? Their living arrangements? A job? Marriage and children of their own?

In Australia we have the National Disability Insurance Scheme, which is a taxpayer funded government scheme that allows Sarah and people like her to live an independent life. Sarah has a package which gives her 24-hour support and so she can live in her own unit, supported by a team of support workers—all young women around her own age—who teach her life skills and support her in all that she does.

There are non-verbal people just like Sarah who lead very meaningful lives and are productive members of society. For example, there is the Brotherhood of the Wordless (BOW)[56] who are a unique group of writers and poets with impaired ability to communicate, based in Brisbane. Knowing people like this exist and are thriving gives me so much hope for Sarah's life. What I want for my daughter is to reach her full potential and unlock all her God-given talents. I believe she is highly intelligent and can do great things with her life. It is a matter of time and having people around who believe in her potential and who can connect her with like-minded others.

---

[56] http://brotherhoodofthewordless.com/ accessed July 2020

It is also my hope she can have a partner who she loves and who loves her. I do not believe Sarah could cope with having children of her own and she will continue to always need some support.

What are/have been the joys of raising your child?

Sarah being able to communicate with me using her pictures and facilitated communication has been one of the greatest joys. When Sarah was 18, she met with and had a conversation (via a communication device) with a young man who was also non-verbal. He would type what he wanted to say into this device, press a button and what he had typed would be translated into speech. He would then pass the device to Sarah and she would type her answer to him. One of the things this young man communicated to Sarah was that she had a pretty smile and to see her sweet reaction was pure joy. He also asked her "Is it good being autistic?" and Sarah's response was "No". This conversation gave me an amazing insight into Sarah's mind. Knowing that she understands and has the ability to communicate is one of the highlights of my life.

It also gives me great joy to know Sarah loves me and to hear her say what sounds like "Mum". I love getting to know her quirky personality and it is so good being able to joke around with her. Seeing Sarah in her own unit and making such solid progress, despite all the challenges she still faces, has been a joy. She is a great girl.

What are/have been the hardest challenges raising your child?

There have been so many challenges during the years of raising my daughter. In her younger years, keeping her safe was a huge challenge. Sarah went through a phase where she escaped from the house twice, and got to the end of our street, but thankfully our neighbours brought her back safe. From then on, we made sure we always deadlocked the house from the inside. If we were out and about, she could take off so quickly and run like a rocket, once going headfirst straight into a fountain. She could not swim at the time, but I was right behind her and scooped her out before any damage could be done. I ended up getting a wrist strap for Sarah, to keep her safe when we were out.

When she was growing up, Sarah did not have any real friends. If she invited other children to her birthday party, they usually attended, and once or twice she was invited to theirs, but the reality was that most children did not want to get to know Sarah. I would often feel so sad for her in those situations and was grateful whenever people made a genuine effort to include her in conversations and try to get to know her.

As a young teenager, her most challenging times were when she would strip naked in front of others, which was mortifying for me as I tried vainly to preserve her dignity. It was also hard navigating her getting her period and finding the right sanitary protection. She would rip sanitary pads out of her underwear, and this was difficult with regards to hygiene. I looked online for an alternative, settling on period pants available from websites like Loveluna.com[57] and Modibods[58] so Sarah did not have to worry about pads and tampons. Now, as an adult, she will wear pads without any problems.

Due to Sarah's oral sensitivities, brushing her teeth was always a huge challenge. We trialled many toothbrushes—electric, one with three heads, a baby toothbrush—to find a suitable one. Sarah needs a general anaesthetic to get a good clean and any dental work done. Getting blood

---

[57] https://www.loveluna.com/

[58] https://www.modibodi.com/ all accessed July 2020

tests and X-rays were always difficult but as Sarah gets older, these things do get easier. Sarah has sensory challenges with clothing—these must be of soft material and she prefers shirts with sleeves, pants, and shorts, rather than dresses. Shoes must be runners and slip-ons. Her hair has in the past had to be cut by me (very quickly) while she was standing up, but now Sarah is able to sit in a chair with a towel around her shoulders while her hair is cut. We are hopeful that she will one day be able to get her hair done at the hairdressers. Sarah can also now tolerate having her hair put into a ponytail or bun, which is a big accomplishment and shows the progress she is making.

Finding the right medication and the correct dosage also presented challenges for Sarah. A couple of times we had to get her off certain medications because of the side-effects—for example, she would be drooling, zoned out or making odd twisting movements with her body, or smashing her head against the concrete. Sarah never slept for three days coming off one lot of medications and thankfully I was able to get her into respite for that time. The emotional toll during those times was huge because I knew Sarah was in deep anguish, but I was not equipped to help her, and she could not accept comfort from me.

Sarah needs help with wiping after going to the toilet, as well as needing prompting to hand wash. When Sarah was little, she would constantly smear faeces over the floor and walls and so keeping her hands clean was almost impossible. This presented big problems when she attended respite. She used to attend one place daily, so I could work, and they eventually withdrew support because her hygiene and other behaviours became too challenging. A meeting was called, and I was given a document with all the carers' thoughts about Sarah and me, about how they thought Sarah needed so much help and that I did not take them seriously. My reality was that I was barely existing at that time, so overwhelmed by my life and trying to juggle everything at once, and I simply could not cope with trying to find a solution to Sarah's

HOW DO I DO THIS?

challenging behaviours. I had put Sarah into the care of the people at this support organisation, believing they were the experts and could implement solutions. I could not know (because they did not tell me until that meeting) that my daughter's behaviour was too challenging for them and endangered other children at the respite house.

It is extremely painful to come to a place where you cannot see how your child's challenges will ever be addressed and you cannot see how their life is ever going to progress to a level where they are off survival mode. Sometimes I would wish Sarah had a physical disability, like being in a wheelchair, rather than a sensory one like autism—because it was so hard to help her cope and keep her balanced. It was at times such a dark, dark, desolate place where there was only paralysing despair and utter desperation.

I learned to be hypervigilant when Sarah was in public. If we were out and about in public at a shopping centre, it was hard to witness the stares and whispers from some people when Sarah would make her loud, guttural noises. Most people were kind and understanding, but I used to mentally "put my blinkers on" and just try to get through situations. Sarah could have a severe meltdown from sensory overload or randomly attack someone. One example was when Sarah was about ten years old and I took her to McDonald's. It was quiet in the play area, which was hugely important for Sarah, as there was less chance of an incident if there were only a few people around. I let Sarah go in and play, and she went to the top of the enclosed slide (it was like a tunnel). There was another little girl up there and it turned out that Sarah was not moving down the slide (sometimes Sarah's brain was not successful in relaying the message to her body that she *could* move), and this little girl wanted to have a turn. Sarah pulled this girl's hair so hard that a chunk of it came out. I had to go up the slide and get Sarah down and apologise profusely to the girl and her Mum, who was understanding about the whole incident. After that, I avoided any enclosed play areas and always made sure Sarah was in plain view wherever she was.

It horrified me that Sarah could do these things and I would feel so ashamed and so angry. I knew it was the autism and her sensory issues, but I still felt so bad that Sarah could not be like other children and that she had so much difficulty coping in the real world. Over the years, I have learned to know the signals or "whispers" when Sarah is getting stressed. Her eyes start to look a bit glazed and her expression gets strained. Often, she will pick at her lip, or her arm or just below her knee. Sometimes she picks at her toenails and has picked them completely off on occasion. It is when I have chosen to ignore these signals that things can turn ugly.

The possibility of Sarah flipping into a meltdown and attacking herself, us and others was always very real and close. Often, we did not have the least idea what caused this. Was it a shadow on the wall? Was Sarah in pain anywhere? Were her clothes not fitting right? Was there a noise or a smell that set her off? Many times, we had to call the ambulance and the police and Sarah would go to the Outpatients Department and be sedated and monitored. On one occasion, Sarah ripped the flesh from her wrists with her teeth, and there was nothing we could do other than call the ambulance. To feel utterly powerless to help or comfort my child was completely devastating to me. Sarah is incredibly strong and sometimes it took six male ambulance officers to match her in strength and help her calm down. These wonderful people helped us in so many ways and got us through an extremely hard time in our lives. Acceptance and non-judgment are such a relief when you have a child with special needs.

Thinking how it must be to live in Sarah's skin and how she has been misunderstood and shunned for most of her life is incredibly challenging. It breaks my heart. Once she had a severe meltdown in the street because we needed to find a toilet quickly and I misread her signals. She started to attack me, and the police saw this and wanted to arrest her. I had to explain the situation to them, and after finding a toilet, we sat in the back of their police van (a nice, quiet enclosed space which was very calming for Sarah) with me telling them about the challenges of her autism. They shared that they were never given any training on how to handle the challenges of people like Sarah. By the end of our conversation, Sarah had calmed down and they could see she was not a threat.

It was challenging to see Sarah making progress in mastering certain skills but then, without warning, this progress would be gone. It was like the signals in her brain would fire and connect to build a neural pathway one day, but then the next day the signal would misfire, and the connection would be lost.

Sarah's obsessions made it hard to keep the house looking cosy and inviting. She could never tolerate any paintings on the walls, and I learned to hide the photo albums because she would take all the photos and tear little pieces off the edges until the photos were virtually gone. Sarah went through a long stage of being obsessed with Coles catalogues to ease her anxiety. She would rip them into little pieces and store them in a special box but nowadays, as she is not as anxious, she does not tend to do this as much.

What has your child taught you?

In so many ways, Sarah has been the making of me, and I have learned so much through being her mother. She has taught me that I can advocate for her and that I must never let go of trying to give her the best life possible. Sarah has taught me how to be patient. She has taught me that non-verbal does not mean non-intelligence and that there are many ways we as human beings can communicate with each other. Sarah has taught me how to love in a way that I could never have comprehended before becoming her mother. Her courage and bravery in the face of huge challenges is an inspiration to me. Sarah was born on Anzac Day and I often refer to her as my "old soldier" because she has fought so many battles in her young life and, each and every day, she overcomes so much just to be in our world.

How do you view your child's special needs?

At first, I saw these as being a difficulty that needed to be overcome and I believed this could be done through nutritional and biomedical intervention. I would read about other children recovering in this way and I must have spent thousands of dollars over the years on supplements and made Sarah take so many tablets in the hope she would be helped (she could not tolerate these with water, so I used to put them on a spoonful of peanut butter or yoghurt). Now Sarah takes zinc, magnesium, B12 spray, fish oil and probiotics, with a low dose of Epilim (for absence seizures) and a minimal dose of Risperidone to calm her and help her function more easily.

I now see Sarah's special needs as being part of her unique personality and I accept her for who she is—a beautiful and amazing young woman. She has an incredible memory and can recall things from years ago, which she very adeptly looks up on You Tube. Sarah is extremely sensitive, and she can pick up on a person's emotions as soon as they enter a room—if someone came into a room angry or upset then they would have to be prepared for Sarah to mirror this back to them. Her hearing is super sensitive also. I am excited to think about the future potential and possibilities for Sarah, now that she is an adult and has great support from a team of people who believe in her abilities and potential.

HOW DO I DO THIS?

What would you say to other parents of special needs children just beginning their journey? What advice/suggestions would you have for them?

I would say to be kind to yourself and realise you cannot do everything for your child. You are not alone in this and do not be too proud or too ashamed to get the help you need. You have nothing to be ashamed of—shame serves no purpose whatsoever and is a condemning and minimising mantle to wear. I think because I was in domestic violence, I was conditioned to feel ashamed and this filtered through to Sarah. Get help not only from professionals, but also from people who have children like yours. I have met some wonderful people face-to-face through our local carers group, through Sarah's schools, as well as online through Facebook.

I would say always trust your own instinct and do what works for you. Your child is not needing to be "fixed"; they have *behaviours* and health challenges that need to be helped. Formulate a good, simple routine and stick to it. Give your child fresh food if possible. I would explain to Sarah how the good food would help her brain work better. This was easy for me to do with Sarah because she did not have food issues, but this is not always the case with other autistic children.

I would also say take courage and use every opportunity to educate people about the nature of a disability like autism. At Sarah's first school we had an information session where her classmates asked me lots of questions about Sarah's special needs—for example, "Was she always like this?" "Why doesn't she talk?" "Is her brain broken?" and this was a wonderful way for them to try to get to know Sarah and understand her behaviour, so they could help to support her in the best possible way.

AGE GROUP 20-30

If you could think of one word to describe being a parent of a child with special needs what would it be?

Resilient.

Any final thoughts?

Sarah is in a great phase of her life now and she has a great support team around her. Her support workers are all young women around her age or a little older. We had a team meeting the other day where we focused on what it would take for Sarah to be living her best life. When asked if she had any questions about anything that had been discussed, Sarah typed "Can I change?" Of course, we encouraged her that the answer to this was a resounding "Yes" and she is in the place and time now where this can happen.

If you are the parent of a younger child, I would say to you that the journey does get easier as your child grows and matures. Many of Sarah's more challenging behaviours are gone now and even if they were to return one day in the future, she has a good team around her, and she is learning strategies to help her to cope.

As soon as you can, make the plans for when you are no longer around and get everything legally sorted. After my younger daughter left home to attend University, it was just me and Sarah living together, and I was asked the question "What if your daughter found you dead on the floor one day? What would she do?" That was a very sobering thought, and I knew I had to make arrangements for Sarah. I came to a point in my life where I knew I could no longer care for her properly and give her the life she needed. It was a long process to find a unit and for Sarah to move out of the family home, and I found it hard to let her go, but I am confident that this is the best thing for us all. Sarah is happy to "learn

HOW DO I DO THIS?

how to be an adult" (her words) and, when my time comes, she will not have to cope with finding a new place to live on top of losing me.

I am also Sarah's legal guardian and advocate. In Australia, this is not an automatic thing after your child turns 18. Here in Queensland, I had to go through QCAT[59] and fill out an application and attend a hearing for guardianship to be granted.

Despite all the tests that showed Sarah has "deficiencies" I know that she is not her disability. She has ongoing challenges and issues, but this does not detract from the fact that she is "fearfully and wonderfully made"[60], she is very special and has gifts and talents far beyond what is considered normal in this world.

Please list any organisations in your country that you have found helpful.

Sarah is supported by:

- PoDDSS https://poddss.com.au/ and
- Tipacl – a small community organisation in Townsville that supports people with disability in a way that reflects their individual needs and lifestyle http://tipacl.com.au/
- National Disability Insurance Scheme https://www.ndis.gov.au/

---

[59] Queensland Civil and Administrative Tribunal at https://www.qcat.qld.gov.au accessed July 2020

[60] Psalm 139:14, Holy Bible

AGE GROUP 20-30

- Autism Queensland https://autismqld.com.au/
- Carers Queensland https://carersqld.com.au/

Therapists:

- **Sensory Training and Behaviour Specialists:** Ann Greer and Joyce-Lyn Smith, PoDDSS https://poddss.com.au/
- **Speech Therapist:** Joshua Smith, SPOTs

Books

- *"The Brain That Changes Itself – Stories of Personal Triumph from the Frontiers of Brain Science"* by Norman Doidge, MD
- *"Carly's Voice: Breaking Through Autism"* by Arthur Fleischmann with Carly Fleischmann
- *"Nobody Nowhere: The Remarkable Autobiography of an Autistic Girl"* by Donna Williams
- *"Somebody Somewhere"* The Sequel to *"Nobody Nowhere"*, by Donna Williams

Other Resources:

- The work of Dr Wenn Lawson at http://www.buildsomethingpositive.com/wenn/
- The work of Temple Grandin at https://www.grandin.com/
- The work of Gen Jereb at https://shop.sensorytools.net/tjb/index.html

AGE GROUP 30-50

- Lucy and Monica, 30 (autism and intellectual disability), Australia
- Sue and Christopher, 30 (epilepsy and intellectual disability), Australia
- Cathy and Lily, 37 (childhood disintegrative disorder, partial deafness, cerebral palsy), Australia
- Lillian and Melissa, 47 (cerebral palsy), Australia

LUCY AND MONICA (AUSTRALIA)

Introduction:

Firstly, let me introduce myself. My name is Lucy Rizzini, nee Bedoschi. I have two beautiful daughters—Amy Marie, born in October 1986 and Monica Louise, born March 13, 1990. Monica is my special girl; she has autism and intellectual disability. We live in Townsville, North Queensland, Australia.

HOW DO I DO THIS?

Was it always apparent to you that your child had special needs? If not, when did you notice that something was "different" about your child?

Monica was born by C-section and she was a beautiful, dark-haired baby. She fed well, slept well, and was walking by 14 months. I do remember she had some funny little ways, but I did not think anything was amiss with Monica. I just thought she did things slower and hit her milestones later than her sister Amy. Amy reached her milestones early—for example, she was walking at 10 months.

When I took Monica for her two-year assessment to Child Clinic, the nurse there thought she was not reaching her milestones at all. And that is when my nightmare all started.

If you have received a formal diagnosis for your child's special needs, when did this happen? Do you remember what feelings you experienced at the time and was the diagnosis a hard thing to come to terms with? Have you come to terms with it?

When Monica was around two years of age, my GP referred her to a paediatrician. She had occupational therapy, speech therapy and physiotherapy testing, as well as an MRI. The following year Monica also underwent a CT brain scan and chromosome analysis including banding, hearing tests, blood tests, skin nerve tests (no neurocutaneous lesions or abnormalities) and liver and spleen tests (no hepatosplenomegaly). All these tests returned normal results.

A detailed fundoscopy showed no specific neurological disease and no clues to an underlying aetiology (the cause or set of causes of a disease or condition). So, Monica's tests were all "normal", but we knew there was something terribly wrong with our little girl! The paediatrician stated that we may never have a precise aetiological explanation for Monica's mental disability, for which he seemed reluctant to place a label. He called it mental retardation and I hated that term. It was horrible! A disability sounds nicer, but did it really matter? All I knew is we had to do everything we could to help our little girl!

In a letter dated August 29, 1995, Monica's paediatrician diagnosed autism. He did this more for her sake, so she could get all the help she needed at school, but he was not concerned and did not believe autism was the correct diagnosis for Monica.

I remember feeling totally devastated, as though my whole world had come crashing down. The feeling that your child has a disability is like grieving the loss of what would have been. It was so overwhelming, and my tears would flow freely at random for my beautiful little girl. It was most certainly one of the hardest things I have ever had to deal with. As to whether I have come to terms with Monica's disability, I think I have—to an extent. But I do not think I will ever get over it.

What I worry about all the time is what is going to happen to Monica when I am no longer around. That is always on my mind. I know her sister Amy will check on her and Monica's three little nieces will (I hope) also check on her when I am no longer around. But I am doing the best I can to prepare Monica for when that day comes.

Did you research about how to help your child? What did you do? Which organisations/professionals did you reach out to?

So, we embarked on the journey to help and do whatever we could to help our precious little girl who we love so dearly.

HOW DO I DO THIS?

When I first knew there was a problem, I turned to medical books looking for answers. We reached out to get help from Monica's doctors, paediatrician, speech therapists, occupational therapists, and physiotherapists.

There were meetings all the time. For me, it felt like I was there by myself with a team of professionals telling me things I hardly understood. All the tests were overwhelming, and the results that came back were all low—communication—low; daily living skills—mild to low; social skills—low; motor skills—low. Was there anything good in these tests?

Monica had an Early Special Education Advisory Teacher (E.A.S.A.T) who would come to our house and go through things to help me/us do the best we could at home to help Monica. There was also an ascertainment process in place to help support Monica. She had an Individual Education Plan (I.E.P.), with a Visiting Advisory Teacher for Autism to implement this in the classroom and give the staff support. Monica had a teacher's aide, occupational therapy support for help with her fine motor skills, speech Therapy and physiotherapy. These services were provided by visiting teachers who would see Monica at the school. I usually attended these sessions and all of them helped immensely in putting us on the right track to help Monica. They always had information sheets we could read.

We also learned Makaton signing to help Monica. She picked them up well, so we embarked on improving Monica's skills.

What therapies did/do you use? What routines did you find helpful for your child?

We had already started Monica's therapy with her early intervention plan. We used occupational therapy, speech therapy and physiotherapy.

Like I said, in the beginning I/we did lots of things with Monica with the programs we were given to use. I was Monica's therapist in all areas at home—becoming her speech/occupational/physiotherapist, as well as her Mum and her carer. Sometimes, her Dad and Amy would also do home sessions with Monica.

Every week, there was a therapy session to attend. In those days, I worked full-time at the local hospital and during my lunch break I would usually take Monica to her group speech lesson. We also had occupational therapy trips to Townsville, an hour's drive away, as well as speech lessons and I.E.P. Meetings. It was never ending. On and on.

How as having a child with special needs affected your family? Your marriage? Your other children?

It certainly was not easy having a child with a disability. Nothing was easy! A simple outing could turn into a disaster, sometimes ending with Monica screaming and having a meltdown. We would just go home most times. Amy was always so good with her and she never complained about Monica. They played together and annoyed each other, just like other siblings. I always made sure I was there for Amy too, supporting her whenever I was needed, and I feel we did well in that area.

As for myself, little did I realise that my health was being affected and in May of 1994, I had a nervous breakdown. I just could not cope any longer. It was horrible and it took me years to totally recover. But I did everything to get better because I had to look after my daughters and husband. I was terrified of a relapse and ended up going part-time at work, five days per fortnight.

As the years went by, it did take its toll on my marriage. I was never the same after that breakdown and Steve became more and more unhappy and just wanted out. So, in July 2005 he left the family home. It was not easy on my own with Monica, but I would never be without her. Amy was away at university and came home on weekends. Monica would go to her Dad's for sleepovers. I had free time then and I did not know what to do with myself! Steve moved south for work but always came back to visit and we ended up working things out. He continued to work away from home every month and it was difficult, but we managed. I just kept trying; just to help my girl.

How do you take care of yourself? What self-care strategies do you use and how have you been able to implement them?

After the breakdown, I was not getting better so my doctor sent me to a psychologist, a psychiatrist, and a social worker. I had regular visits until I was mentally well enough to go on without doctor's visits. I was put on medication, had lots of counselling and I read material that would help me. I used to listen to relaxation tapes all the time. The days I worked I had half-an-hour for lunch, and I would go home, lay on the bed, and listen to my tapes. It was great when I no longer needed them. I just wanted to be okay for my girls! It just took time, but I got there.

But oh, what horrible feelings when I was ill. The fear of having a panic attack was very intense—I couldn't watch things on TV because they scared me; I couldn't go for a simple walk on the beach because the movement of the waves made me feel sick; and going on family or a holiday and doing everyday things were so overwhelming. I was so glad as time passed to get better and better. It took years. Years. I never totally got over it; to this day I am unable to go without medication. But that is okay; I am happy and that is what counts.

AGE GROUP 30-50

Do you have a faith? If so, how has this helped you cope with life with your child?

I am a Catholic. I prayed and prayed a lot when I was unwell. I used to go to church with the girls and it always felt good to do so. I would pray for the girls and this was a comfort for Monica. But I no longer attend church.

How important/necessary is your family support or the support of your friends/networks? Do you feel as though you have enough support?

Steve and I would take turns to have a break for a few hours, but an hour later I would be home as I could not stay away from my girls. My Mum had passed away just before Monica's first birthday and I only have one older sister, and there was *never* any support from her. She never offered to take the girls for a break—maybe she was scared? I don't know. I had friends but none that would offer much support, maybe for a couple of hours sometimes. It was extremely hard not to have anyone to say "Bring the girls over" so I could have a break.

There is a respite house in our town so that was where Monica would go. As she got older, she hated going there and would usually not eat nor co-operate with staff. Monica would only be happy if there was a certain staff member working. If I were at work and Monica was at respite, I would be worried every minute of the day and that was hard. Everything was *so hard*. So, it was just usually just me, her Dad and Amy. A special carer took her home for a sleepover a couple of times. To this day, even though they do not see each other so much, they have an extraordinarily strong bond and the love is there.

HOW DO I DO THIS?

What do you hope/think the future holds for your child? Their living arrangements? A job? Marriage and children of their own?

All I hope for is that Monica is happy and able to cope and live in supported care, where she is coming up to her six-year anniversary in November 2020. This was by far the hardest thing I have ever had to do. Bucket loads of tears were shed when a placement came up in Townsville and Monica left home to live there. She was so miserable and depressed living with three other girls—all so different—in one house. It broke my heart to see Monica so unhappy and I could have taken her home a million times. It was extremely hard, but we persevered with the situation.

Two years ago, Monica was able to move to a new house and now lives with one other housemate. This is a much better place for Monica and most of the time she is happy. She has wonderful support workers and she goes on outings and is enjoying herself.

I am unsure how Monica would go with a job; she might be able to stay on track with help from her support workers. As much as it breaks my heart, I know my beautiful girl will not ever get married or have any children of her own. This is part of the grieving process for a parent; what we have lost for Monica. But so long as she is happy, it is okay. I do often wonder what she is thinking and whether she realises any of this?

What are/have been the joys of raising your child?

Monica loves to laugh and make a game of things and have a bit of fun. Over the years, she has developed a wicked, funny sense of humour that is the best! When she was growing up, we would be forever joking around and making things fun and a bit silly.

Our girl is certainly unique, but then all children are unique. I/we embrace her with all the love we can give—she is our beautiful, loving girl.

It has been a great joy seeing Monica achieve things—however small, they were like a mountain to us.

What are/have been the hardest challenges raising your child?

Getting Monica to co-operate was the hardest challenge. I would be trying to get her to do something, but if she did not want to, there was no way she would give in. If Monica did not want to get in the car, she would not get in. I think I was always late for work and the girls were always late for school. So sometimes, I would say "Okay, we're going now, goodbye Monica!!" We would do a short drive around the block. "Are you ready to get in the car now?" It usually worked.

Another of the hardest challenges was when Monica would have a meltdown in public. The stares and the looks from others were the worst. You felt like saying something but usually bit your tongue.

To help with the challenges, we used strategies that were taught to us. Time out was used, as well as just being consistent. We would praise the good things Monica did and, wherever possible, ignore the bad.

What has your child taught you?

My child has taught me to love in a way I never thought possible and to be patient more than I knew possible. There were some really difficult days and goodness knows what was going on in Monica's mind! She has most certainly taught me to be resilient. Hard as it may have been, she has taught me to toughen up. At times, there was so much stress and so many setbacks, but I always seemed to find a way to cope and just get on with things. Over the years, there were many buckets of tears shed. Emotional strength is especially important, so look after number one! You! Learn to take time out.

We must learn many things to care for our children. One of these is becoming their advocate, especially if we are no longer looking after our children and they are living in supported care like Monica. This is extremely important because who will be their voice otherwise, especially if they cannot speak for themselves? Amy and I are advocates for Monica. If family cannot be involved, then a legal guardian can step in to ensure all the person's interests are taken care of.

How do you view your child's special needs?

I do not think of Monica's special needs as a disability. Because no matter what, I love her more than anything and would do anything for her. I look more at the things she has achieved and how far we have come. Believe me, there were hills to climb up and down.

I/we stood by her and helped her in every way possible. We did what the therapists suggested to us to help her achieve to the best of her ability. It was a long hard road to achieve little things, but you seem to forget the bad times and just admire and be pleased for where Monica is now. We are just so happy for her, to see how far she has come. It is amazing.

What would you say to other parents of special needs children just beginning their journey? What advice/suggestions would you have for them?

Just do whatever you can to help your child achieve, to the best of their ability. Love them with all the love you can give. Be there for them. Take them to their therapy sessions and do what the therapists ask you to do at home for them, with them. Teach your child to do as much as they can achieve for themselves. It may take longer, but consistency is the key. Never give up.

Make sure you look after yourself first and foremost. Take whatever time you can to do things you enjoy. It will help you immensely to cope with the stress of caring for your disabled child—if you go down, what is going to happen? You are number one. As hard as it may be to leave your child in care for a weekend now and then, just do it. It will save your sanity.

If you could think of one word to describe being a parent of a child with special needs what would it be?

Eggshells!

Tread lightly—because you never know what is coming next. It is not easy, and some days will be better than others. Go with it.

Just love them with all your heart. You will find a love—a special love you never thought possible.

HOW DO I DO THIS?

Any final thoughts?

Even though the road gets rough just keep going, you will get there. You will come across some amazing support workers and some who are not so amazing. They are the ones who make things harder for you and your child.

When Monica first went into care, we had some extremely tough times through problems with some staff. I was at my wits end. I would visit Monica and sometimes the state I would find her in was disgusting and the staff would say it was because she refused to eat or shower. Monica had lost weight and was so depressed. She would have bruises on her arms from getting hit and punched by other housemates, but the staff would say it was Monica who was the one who lashed out, pinching, and grabbing. We would ask "Why was she doing this?" I know my daughter and I knew there had to be a reason for Monica to act out and that she would not do that for nothing. My poor girl!

The staff would say that her other housemates were not doing anything wrong and so it was always Monica's fault. It was a nightmare. At one stage, staff had me believing I had done everything wrong just because I had done everything for Monica and so now, she could not do anything for herself. I probably made mistakes but so does everyone else. I would ring up sometimes to check on Monica and one staff member would pretend the phone was playing up and hang up on me (funny thing, it never happened again after she left). The support staff at the time did not care or realise the pain I was going through and the anguish I felt for Monica. I could see how sad she was when I would visit. I was a mess! I also was not coping with my Monica having left home. It was the worst time of my life.

It took a few years, but things seem much better these days. My daughter is happy, and I feel happy that she is okay. There are still some little ups and downs, but we made it. Monica turns 30 this year (2020). I still check how she is going every day, twice a day. She comes home for visits and for weekends. I will continue to do this for as long as I am able to.

Monica and I have an incredibly special bond and I love her to bits.

So, give it your all, and never, never give up.

Cheers!

Please list any organisations in your country that you have found helpful.

- National Disability Insurance Scheme (NDIS) https://www.ndis.gov.au

- Uniting Care Disability Support Services https://www.uniting.org/services/disability-services

- Endeavour Foundation https://www.endeavour.com.au

- Aruma Disability Services https://www.aruma.com.au

- Alliance Speech Pathology Therapy https://alliancerehab.com.au

- Education, Therapy and Support Services – Autism Queensland · https://autismqld.com.au

- Office of the Public Guardian https://www.publicguardian.qld.gov.au

SUE AND CHRISTOPHER (AUSTRALIA)

Introduction:

My name is Sue. I am the sole carer of my son Christopher, 30, who has been diagnosed with a severe intellectual disability and epilepsy. We currently live in Townsville, Queensland, Australia.

Chris is my middle child—luckily for us he does not suffer from Middle Child Syndrome[61]! My elder son Steven is 33 and a pharmacist, currently living on the Sunshine Coast and my daughter Amy is 28 and a nurse, also living in Townsville.

Was it always apparent to you that your child had special needs? If not, when did you notice that something was "different" about your child?

The first time we were aware that something may have been wrong with Chris was when I was asked by the paediatrician at the hospital whether Chris looked like a member of the family. He was concerned that Chris may have had a chromosome abnormality: i.e. Down Syndrome. Blood tests were done to identify any abnormality and they came back negative.

Having Steven already, who was then three, we were able to gauge milestones and we soon realised that there was something different

---

[61] https://www.urbandictionary.com/define.php?term=Middle%20Child%20Syndrome accessed May 2020

about Chris. He was reaching the milestones much later; he was around 12 months when he began to roll on the floor and start to crawl, and over two years of age when he started to walk. This made life extremely difficult as I had our last baby, Amy, by then.

Chris was also demonstrating signs of self-stimulation—staring at his hand, shaking his hands wildly and performing certain actions continuously, which could only be stopped by intervention. We had no idea these actions were self-stimulatory, and we were allowing Chris to do these things. It was only after receiving a visit from an occupational therapist that we were told we needed to intervene and stop these behaviours. At the time, we were living in Wangaratta, which is a small country town, and this made any form of specialist care especially difficult to procure.

If you have received a formal diagnosis for your child's special needs, when did this happen? Do you remember what feelings you experienced at the time and was the diagnosis a hard thing to come to terms with? Have you come to terms with it?

Intellectual disability is a hard thing to diagnose because the only test is gauging the stages of development.

With regards to his epilepsy, Chris had his first seizure at eight months, and it lasted for 30 minutes. On arrival at Wangaratta District Base Hospital this was diagnosed as a febrile seizure[62] (a convulsion in a child caused by a spike in body temperature) and no further action was taken.

---

[62] https://www.ninds.nih.gov/Disorders/Patient-Caregiver-Education/Fact-Sheets/Febrile-Seizures-Fact-Sheet

HOW DO I DO THIS?

Eight weeks later, on a visit to the Melbourne Zoo, Chris experienced his second seizure. We stripped him down and rushed him to The Royal Children's Hospital in Melbourne, which was close by. This seizure was recorded as a nonfebrile seizure[63]. The Children's Hospital did thorough tests on Chris and he was diagnosed with epilepsy[64] at that time.

I remember feeling completely devastated by this diagnosis because of the way in which it was delivered. This was done publicly, during the evening mealtime in the Children's Ward packed with parents waiting to assist their children. The opportunity to grieve this diagnosis privately had been stolen from us. I needed to somehow try and process the ramifications of this diagnosis in my head. This was so difficult under the circumstances, and I remember just laying my head on Chris's bed.

For the rest of my life, I will never forget this moment.

What therapies did/do you use? What routines do you find helpful for your child?

Chris accesses SpeechEase Speech Therapy[65] and has an excellent speech therapist who has been fabulous in gauging the best learning experience for him. Chris tried technology application Proloquo2Go[66] and Tools2Talk[67], but the screens were too confusing for Chris. We are

---

[63] http://www.sienapediatrics.com/SeizuresWithoutFever.pdf

[64] https://www.betterhealth.vic.gov.au/health/conditionsandtreatments/epilepsy all accessed May 2020

[66] https://www.assistiveware.com/products/proloquo2go

[67] https://apps.apple.com/au/app/tools2talk-create-your-own-communication-aids-and-chat/id1074982035 both accessed May 2020

now using picture photo books which have step-by-step pictures to perform tasks.

Chris is a very easy-going young man and adjusts to situations easily; therefore, we have not followed routines in the regimented way that I hear some people require.

Chris accesses two support agencies and workers attend our home and help him with personal care and to access the community. They are mostly young men as Chris does not have a regular male role model in his life.

Did you research about how to help your child? What did you do? Which organisations/professionals did you reach out to?

As I mentioned earlier, at the time of Chris's diagnosis our family was living in Wangaratta, where specialists and services were quite minimal.

Chris saw a paediatrician regularly who prescribed his epilepsy medication and kept the levels monitored through blood tests. Chris also saw an occupational therapist and attended a Special School playgroup which offered stimulation and exercises. This also gave the Mums a chance to network and learn from one another.

When Chris was four years old, we moved to Townsville and continued his paediatric support and monitoring of his medication levels with Dr Pat Ryan. Every year he was under Dr Ryan, Chris would attend Townsville General Hospital to have an electroencephalogram (EEG); a medical test used to measure the electrical activity of the brain. It took years before Townsville attained a permanent neurologist at the General Hospital. This made Chris's assessment and medication monitoring limited to a GP who did not really have the specialist skills required for a thorough epilepsy monitoring and programming.

Thanks to the newly introduced NDIS Package Chris has recently undergone a Neuropsychological Assessment through North Queensland Neuropsychology Service. This is something I recommend to people as this agency has delved into Chris's complete medical history and supplied our family with an exceptionally thorough report with a complete overview from his birth to the present day.

This report will help Chris in his application and review for the NDIS.

How has having a child with special needs affected your family? Your marriage? Your other children?

As a family, we have adjusted to life a little differently than a regular family would. It is a certainty that Chris's diagnosis meant that life as we knew it would never be the same, but we have all adjusted and accepted our lives and have come to terms with this.

In the early years, it was harder because Chris had more self-stimulatory behaviours, but through the years, life has become much easier. This is because Chris's behaviours are now very minimal and as the other children grew and matured, they did not require as much supervision as when they were little.

Chris certainly added some extra strains on our family; however, I do not believe this was the reason for our 30-year marriage falling down. Chris's Dad was not really equipped to deal with the stresses of life in general. He was happy to leave everything for me to organise and so I was the parent responsible for all things other than bringing in the weekly income. I think the strain of looking after my family with a man who was happy to "put his head in the sand" took its toll on me.

Neither one of us were happy and had drifted apart in every way—emotionally, spiritually, and physically. Once our children became more independent, I felt it was time to take a leap of faith and take up the responsibility on my own—after all, I was doing everything anyway apart from bringing in the money.

I believe the separation was the hardest on our youngest daughter Amy, who had just begun High School. Our elder son had just begun University and seemed to have the understanding that it was better for his parents to part ways and have a chance of happiness. At the time of our separation, Chris's Dad was living in Townsville and the kids would visit him every weekend. A few years later he relocated to the Sunshine Coast and we agreed that Chris would join him once he had settled into his new life.

Unfortunately for Chris, I think his Dad had a taste of the good life and freedom and I realised he was not interested in supporting Chris in a living capacity. In the beginning, he visited Townsville regularly but then the visits became less and less frequent. This really took its toll on Chris and still does. It is heartbreaking that someone could love another as much as Chris loves his Dad, and for his Dad to completely lack the capacity to appreciate that unconditional love.

I would walk over broken glass if someone loved me that much!

How do you take care of yourself? What self-care strategies do you use and how have you been able to implement them?

I am quite poor at looking after myself and I have in fact become a little depressed at not having the freedom to do things I used to like. I used to exercise daily and watch my weight and diet, but I do not really worry about this now.

Psychologically, I think it is easier for me to accept that my time is not my own, that I am tied as a single mother and totally reliant on support workers for a chance of some free time. Please do not misunderstand me, I would not change my situation for anything. Being a sole carer does have its setbacks—lack of freedom being one of them—but as I grow older this is becoming easier to accept and it does not have the same emotional hold over me anymore.

I do drink alcohol much more than I should and as I am by nature a loner there is no one around me to hold me accountable for this.

I joined Toastmasters[68], a public speaking group, which has given me a chance to claim myself for a short time; to clear away the cobwebs and use my imagination and memory to write an array of different speeches.

Do you have a faith? If so, how has this helped you cope with life with your child?

Through my life, I have come in and out of faith.

As a child I went to St Augustine's Church and attended Sunday School. I remember at some point in my childhood feeling unhappy as I rode my bicycle to Sunday School, and I felt angry at my mother for forcing me to attend.

When I was old enough to make my own decision, I chose not to follow my faith.

During the early years of raising our family I had drawn away from God and thus my children were not baptised and were not encouraged to follow religion. How they feel about faith and God now is something we

---

[68] http://www.toastmasters.org.au accessed May 2020

as a family do not discuss. I know the children's Dad does not have a faith although both his parents were staunch Christians.

I know I am not a Christian, spreading the word of the Lord in the way that true Christians should be doing, but I know deep in my heart that I am a believer.

A saying I read on our local church wall stays with me: "It is not believing you know, it is knowing you believe."

How important/necessary is your family support or the support of your friends/networks? Do you feel as though you have enough support?

My own mother died early, before I had been married or started our family, and this was extremely hard. I did not have my Mum to guide me with her experience, to give that emotional and physical support and her always unconditional love. To add to this, it was hard for me that my children would miss out on knowing one of the best human beings that has ever lived. You may think I write these words with rose-coloured glasses, but everyone who knew my Mum will vouch for my feelings about her.

My wonderful grandmother who we had lived with growing up also passed away when I was pregnant with my first son.

My husband's family were of remarkably similar personalities as Chris's Dad and they truly had an enormous deal of trouble accepting Chris's diagnosis. My father-in-law even said, "If you put a feather in the wind you never know where it will end up". I have never felt so hurt by a sentence and so I realised early on that our family supports were non-existent.

HOW DO I DO THIS?

This made me rely on people around me who were willing to support our family and to love and help me guide our children in the way they so deserved. I remember feeling so alone and scared when I became pregnant that I would look up to the heavens and ask for help. In saying this, I would like to give the biggest shout out to Helen Ross, who supported me like a mother, guiding me in every area of looking after a baby. She loved our children as her own and she was our family's mainstay back then.

As I said before, I am a loner by nature and I have also been very blessed with an abundance of energy, reasonable intellect and an ability to adapt; Lord knows I had learned to adapt from babyhood, through my growing up—throughout my entire life. I have a great deal of experience at adapting to changing situations.

As for the support I have now, Carers Queensland had a local branch in Townsville organisation with a wonderful and empathetic team who supported carers beautifully. Through accessing their services, I realised early on that the commitment and investment of this team was a true blessing. Unfortunately, the government put this up for tender and Carers Queensland was not chosen. I honestly felt gutted at losing this invaluable team. Over the years, everyone had made a connection and they knew our personalities, our stories, and our struggles. How could we—and why should we—start to make these connections all over again? Wellways has now taken over the responsibility of supporting carers and they have huge shoes to fill, especially in Townsville. Watch this space!

Chris's Dad has not changed his approach to supporting Chris and I think the other children are busy in their own lives; they can only support us emotionally in these times where more education and qualifications are needed to keep their employment. My family and the people around us see me functioning well, running a home, keeping a nice garden, looking after Chris, and still seeming to be happy and on top of life. I liken myself to the duck who appears to be smoothly sailing on the water but non-one can see him madly paddling away underneath.

What do you hope/think the future holds for your child? Their living arrangements? A job? Marriage and children of their own?

The future is something I try not to put too much focus on. I think when Chris was first diagnosed, I felt I was trying to second guess everything. I was a mess and trying to take one day at a time was how I sometimes got through.

So many clichés through this really. I have been a stay at home Mum, and I am still a full-time carer for Chris. I hope to look after him for as long as I can, health permitting. In saying that, I would not be human if I did not do some planning for the future. I plan to sell our home and move down south with Chris to where Steven lives, in the hope that when I can no longer be responsible for Chris, his brother will step up. It is a blessing for us that Steven has already agreed to take on the responsibility for Chris if and when something happens, and I can longer look after Chris. I hope to buy a two-bedroom unit on the Sunshine Coast where Chris will remain with 24-hour support for the rest of his lifetime.

Because Chris is severely intellectually disabled, with epilepsy, and unable to concentrate for any length of time, the prospects of employment and marriage and children of his own are an impossibility. You can call me a defeatist or you can call me a realist; it is what it is.

HOW DO I DO THIS?

What are/have been the joys of raising your child?

Clichés, clichés, and more clichés.

Chris teaches anyone who he meets more about life than any other person and there are blessings a plenty raising a man like Chris. I call him my "Giant Teddy".

Chris's School Guidance Officer once said to me, "You know Sue, you will never have to worry about Chris and his future because his personality is such that anyone who meets him just wants to look out for him". This was music to my ears and to this day it is something that remains with me and gives me enormous comfort.

I think small achievements by Chris and his persistence has taught me a lot about my own approach to situations. He lives in the present moment, is accepting and does not make judgements about anything or anyone. Chris is content 90% of the time and I would say that is better than happiness, although Chris is also extremely happy.

Whenever I find myself on that downward spiral, Chris senses my mood and will laugh out loud. Guess what? That snaps me right out of my thoughts and puts me squarely back in the present moment. He has incredible insight into people, and I sense he can read people's hearts and intentions.

As far as Chris's siblings go, I believe having Chris in our family has helped shape them into the compassionate, understanding and accepting adults that they are today. They are both connected to the health industry. As I mentioned earlier, one is a pharmacist and one is a nurse.

AGE GROUP 30-50

What are/have been the hardest challenges raising your child?

In Wangaratta, when Chris was first diagnosed there was a woman who also had a son who was diagnosed at the same time, but with cerebral palsy. This woman was so adamant on fighting for whatever supports and entitlements she could get for her son that her marriage fell apart soon after her son's diagnosis.

I may have let Chris down in a lot of ways back then, but my main goal was always for us to function as a family and be as "normal" (my least favourite word) as possible. I wanted all our children to be able to access opportunities that were available to them; they needed to be children, albeit children growing up under some extremely difficult circumstances. We really did our best to make our stressful family situation as fun as it could possibly be for them.

The early years of raising our family were incredibly difficult for me and most of the time I felt tied. This feeling has eased with time.

The children's Dad was of the "old school thinking" and believed the responsibility of the father was solely to bring home the money. He worked long hours, and this meant I was basically raising the family on my own. In retrospect, I think the hardest thing was when the other children wanted to be involved in sports. Most of the time I had to rely on others to pick them up and drop them off because Chris just wasn't interested in sitting still to watch a game of cricket or basketball. Sometimes he was so poorly behaved that he embarrassed the kids and it was better to accept our situation. This is where I think I felt it was the hardest on my other children; while other kids had their parents supporting them and cheering them on, our children had to go it alone. Luckily for us, they seem to hold no animosity towards Chris or about some of the parental support they have missed out on.

HOW DO I DO THIS?

Without wanting to sound resentful, you realise your time is not your own, anything you want to do has to be planned and there are so many times you must be prepared for disappointment.

I remember when Chris was scheduled for respite some weekends and he would out and out refuse to go and there was nothing anyone could do. I remember driving back home with Chris in the car crying my eyes out because I knew there would be no respite until the next month.

What has your child taught you?

In fact, our lives are blessed with a young man who offers wonderful life lessons to all of us, living in the moment, accepting everything with no judgement and loving unconditionally. You hear it so many times, but believe me, it is the truth. Chris has taught us incredibly more than we could ever be able to teach him.

How do you view your child's special needs?

I believe Chris has been the cement that holds us as a family unit together, just by being. Yes, we have separated as parents, but the love each one of us has for Chris and each other can never be underestimated. A diagnosis does not mean a life sentence, it just means life will be a little more difficult for you and your family.

AGE GROUP 30-50

What would you say to other parents of special needs children just beginning their journey? What advice/suggestions would you have for them?

My greatest advice for any new parent of a child, regardless of one with special needs, is to take one day at a time. Sure, you need to plan and organise, just try not to second guess the "What ifs?"; face them when they arrive. The old saying "Relax: It may never happen" comes to mind.

The greatest piece of advice given to me by an amazing Guidance Officer when Chris was transitioning into school, was to teach Chris's siblings that they are not responsible for their brother at school and they must be allowed to be children in the playground like the others. Teach them your special child's actions and behaviours are not intended to hurt or disappoint them in any way and they must try hard not to take anything they do personally.

A valuable piece of advice for parents is to try to recognise misdirected anger. I soon realised that I might be angry at one of my other children after an incident with Chris. I saw Chris's Dad yelling at the other kids, sometimes just for walking in the room, when Chris had just done something or misbehaved. This is totally unfair; you must check yourself regularly as to why you are angry and direct that anger accordingly.

Also make sure that you network, join playgroups, ask loads of questions, and do not take no for an answer. That said, do not become obsessed with missing out on services or getting what is on offer; sometimes you have got to let things go. You are human and if you have other children you must not allow their support, guidance, love and needs to be overlooked because you are hellbent on making the best life possible for your special child.

HOW DO I DO THIS?

Finally, look at your child and what they have to offer you and your family; what assets they bring to make up your family unit and rejoice in these assets. For us, this was so easy because Chris is just so lovable.

If you could think of one word to describe being a parent of a child with special needs what would it be?

Adaptable.

Any final thoughts?

Enjoy the present moment, meditate, and talk and talk and talk. Once a Christian therapist told me "The Talking Therapy" has been around since the beginning of time.

In saying all the above, I need to add some personal touches, that make life real so anyone reading this can look forward in a positive way. The thing is, from my own experience you have a future, a future full of appreciation for the simple things in life.

At a time in my life when Chris was two and still not walking, I had a double pram and at that time, 30 years ago, they did not come with off road wheels. Anyone who had to push a double pram back then will know how hard this was. Having a rather heavy two-year-old sitting at the front of the pram caused the rubber on the wheels to frequently slip off and, to add to this, we also had to deal with Chris leaning back and waking up baby Amy a lot of the time. I will never forget these were such trying times, dealing with all of that as well as having a five-year-old in tow. I look back now and have a chuckle about this. I thought this would never have been possible because, on reflection, a lot of the time I felt angry and frustrated with my situation.

AGE GROUP 30-50

I remember having to strap baby Amy in a portable rocker and take her with me wherever I went in the house, because we just had no idea if Chris could or would hurt her. When we were travelling in the car, we had to sit Steven in the middle so Chris would not reach out and touch Amy or wake her up if she were sleeping.

The best part of all these struggles as a family is that Amy and Chris have a wonderful relationship now. Amy teases him and does so with the fondness of a baby sister remembering what she has experienced in her life growing up with a special needs brother. I only know that experience as a parent. Steven calls Amy the quiet achiever. She knew that if something needed to be done, she had to do it herself, because keeping Chris safe was always our priority. When Amy was four nothing she wore ever matched! I must say I was a bit embarrassed, but I think this was the least of our worries, right?

As for my eldest son Steven, the relationship and bond he feels towards Chris is so strong that every year he comes up from the Sunshine Coat to celebrate Chris's birthday. Wouldn't you say this makes us all a very lucky lot?

Any organisations you would recommend?

- North Queensland Neuropsychology Service: https://www.nqns.com.au

- SpeechEase Speech Therapy https://www.speechease.net.au

- Emily's Hope: https://www.ndisproducts.com.au/providers/emily-s-hope-pty-ltd

HOW DO I DO THIS?

- Carer Gateway Support Services (Wellways), replacing Carers Queensland. This is a national support service funded by the Australian Government, providing free support through a network of regional Carer Gateway Service Providers https://www.wellways.org/carers.

- Tipacl Inc. for disability support at http://tipacl.com.au

- Disability Connect Queensland – Department of Communities. https://www.communities.qld.gov.au/disability-connect-queensland

CATHY AND LILY (AUSTRALIA)

Introduction:

I have two adult children and I have raised them as a sole parent since they were nine and eleven years of age. My younger child Lily, now in her late 30s, has multiple disabilities and multiple diagnoses, which have increased over time.

We have always lived in North Queensland.

Was it always apparent to you that your child had special needs? If not, when did you notice that something was "different" about your child?

Lily failed to grow well in utero; she stopped growing for a short period at 20 weeks gestation. At 38 weeks, tests indicated her placenta was functioning inadequately, and so she was delivered. Lily's delivery was straightforward and even though she was rather small, she appeared healthy. Unfortunately, she had a 'cerebral' cry, which is indicative of cerebral irritation. This increased markedly at six weeks, when Lily developed a middle ear infection. We were not in my home city at that time, and the general practitioner we saw did not examine Lily and suggested I should sedate her with Phenergan (an antihistamine with sedative properties). I immediately flew back to my home city where I took her to my regular general practitioner. Her middle ear infection was diagnosed and treated, and Lily was referred to a paediatrician.

HOW DO I DO THIS?

The paediatrician examined my daughter and then referred her for a range of tests, all of which were inconclusive. What we did know was that Lily was small for her age with low muscle tone, she had a small head of which she lacked control, as well as an inability to maintain her body temperature and a high pitched 'cerebral' cry. At the time, the hardest thing was waiting to see how Lily's development progressed and then waiting for the next assessment appointment.

If you have received a formal diagnosis for your child's special needs, when did this happen? Do you remember what feelings you experienced at the time and was the diagnosis a hard thing to come to terms with? Have you come to terms with it?

At six months, Lily was diagnosed with cerebral palsy affecting all four of her limbs; her left side was more affected than her right. At the time, I just wanted to take her to another paediatrician in the hope they would say she was okay.

In addition to her diagnosis, Lily also suffered from multiple middle ear infections, primarily caused by her small head and small Eustachian tubes. When she was sick with a middle ear infection (which was every few weeks), she would become very cerebrally irritable and would projectile vomit; feeding her became an ongoing struggle.

At ten months, Lily was formally diagnosed as partially deaf. She had no hearing in her left ear, but normal hearing in her right. Over time, her hearing has deteriorated, and she now has a moderate loss in her 'good' ear.

At two years and six months, a CT scan revealed Lily had suffered a 'stroke'. This had probably occurred during the second trimester of her gestation, when she stopped growing and was probably caused by maternal Cytomegalo Virus (CMV) infection. CMV is a very mild maternal viral infection but can have devastating effects on the developing foetus. There is no vaccine available.

When Lily was four, she suffered a major seizure, which we hoped (due to her high temperature) was a febrile convulsion. Lily's brain damage meant there was a high risk of epilepsy developing. Six months later, epilepsy was formally diagnosed. I was devastated by this, but looking back, I do not know why I was so upset about this diagnosis.

Over time, Lily's epilepsy has stabilised, but her cognition and physical abilities have continued to deteriorate. She was diagnosed with Childhood Disintegrative Disorder[69]. This is a 'broad brush' diagnosis that covers children with ongoing deterioration in cognitive and physical abilities, without a clear cause identified. Lily's deterioration in skills has been far greater than would be expected from her epilepsy.

Did you research about how to help your child? What did you do? Which organisations/professionals did you reach out to?

Susan's paediatrician consulted with paediatricians in the UK and the USA, as well as throughout Australia, in the hope of finding some interventions that would help. Despite everyone's best intentions, Lily's abilities continue to deteriorate.

Throughout Lily's life, I read and researched all I could. A local support organisation provided weekly therapeutic intervention, and we attended play groups, swimming lessons, childcare and kindergarten to ensure my daughter had as much exposure to support as I could manage. I did a lot of advocacy to facilitate inclusion at kindergarten/childcare and initially

---

[69] https://www.autismag.org/childhood-disintegrative-disorder/ accessed April 2020

HOW DO I DO THIS?

Lily was knocked back because she could not walk very well! Talk about the good old days!

Additionally, Lily had medical interventions and a daily exercise routine to reduce the impact of her cerebral palsy. At 12 months, she was finally able to sit with minimal support. By the time she was two, Lily could outswim all her peers! At two years of age, Lily could stand without support and walk. I also researched and carried out 'patterning' to assist Lily's development and to create new connections within her brain.

Given her subsequent diagnoses I do not know if these interventions have had a long-term beneficial impact, but I do know I did everything possible to ensure the best outcomes for my daughter.

What therapies did/do you use? What routines did/do you find helpful?

At six months of age, Lily was referred for physiotherapy, occupational therapy and speech therapy and she received this support until she went to school. Until she was nine, we paid for private speech therapy. A regular physiotherapy review ensured the exercises/stretches I was doing with my daughter were appropriate and beneficial. I continued the daily stretches until Lily moved into her own unit when she was 36 years old.

Lily also learned Signed English in primary school, and she lip reads very well. This is fortunate because she refuses to wear a hearing aid.

AGE GROUP 30-50

How has having a child with special needs affected your family? Your marriage? Your other children?

Lily's health issues and additional needs has had a huge impact on her brother, as well as on my mental health and financial status. Due to the location centricity of my daughter's support funding prior to the implementation of the NDIS, I was unable to access job opportunities in other states or cities.

I feel it has been an ongoing battle to get support for Lily. When she was young, there was no respite care or family support available. I was a sole parent working full time and studying (essential to maintain my employment) and caring for my other son when I finally received two hours a week of support. Susan could not attend her local school due to her additional needs, so the Education Department provided transport to and from school. At primary school, Lily was able to attend after school care, but this service was not available in high school. When I asked if the transport service could transport her from school to a Family Day Care Provider's home after school I was firmly told 'No' as I should be home in the afternoon to look after my child!!

Now the NDIS has been implemented, life is much easier for me and much improved for my daughter.

How do you take care of yourself? What self-care strategies do you use and how have you been able to implement them?

When my children were living at home I lived in 'survival' mode and somehow managed to survive. Since Lily moved into her own unit, my home life is a lot easier (I no longer have to get up 3–4 times per night!) but she still needs a lot of support.

How important/necessary is your family support or the support of your friends/networks? Do you feel as though you have enough support?

I have wonderful friends, but as my life became more divergent from the more usual path, the more isolated I felt. This is no fault of my friends; it is just how life works.

What do you hope/think the future holds for your child? Their living arrangements? A job? Marriage and children of their own?

Lily now lives independently in her own unit with support funded by the National Disability Insurance Scheme. She enjoys living alone with her cat.

What are/have been the joys of raising your child?

I have met wonderful people who I would never have otherwise met.

What are/have been the hardest challenges raising your child?

In the early years, Lily's epilepsy was difficult to manage. By five years and six months, she was experiencing frequent tonic clonic[70] seizures (the 'drop attacks'). These were so frequent she would 'drop' up to 10 times while she walked across a room. Due to these incessant falls, Lily also had to spend extended periods of time in a stroller. Her tonic clonic

---

[70] https://www.epilepsy.com/learn/types-seizures/tonic-clonic-seizures

seizures continued with frequent episodes of Status Epilepticus[71], but her 'drop attacks' reduced. Academically, Lily was doing quite well at school.

When she was seven, Lily's epilepsy worsened again. She was experiencing frequent partial seizures and tonic clonic seizures, and her cognitive ability deteriorated markedly. Following extensive testing in my home city, Lily was referred to a paediatric neurologist in Sydney. After even more tests it was determined Susan had 'Electrical status in slow wave sleep'[72]. This is a rare epilepsy syndrome and extremely difficult to treat. Despite huge doses of steroids and antiepileptic drugs, Lily's cognition continued to regress.

I found this period of her life incredibly challenging. Lily lost many of her hard-won skills, as well as having difficulty controlling her behaviour. Despite medication and ongoing visits to paediatric neurologists in Sydney and Melbourne, the next five years was a series of worsening, improving and worsening epilepsy and ongoing loss of skills.

When she was around thirteen, Lily experienced yet another marked deterioration and her general health also deteriorated. I was so very fearful she would not survive much longer. However, this was the 'swan song' of my daughter's epilepsy. Lily has not experienced another tonic clonic seizure since, although she continues to experience 'absence' seizures with a marked increase in seizure activity when she is asleep. This ongoing epilepsy has had a devastating impact on her cognitive ability.

---

[71] https://www.epilepsy.com/learn/challenges-epilepsy/seizure-emergencies/status-epilepticus

[72] https://www.epilepsy.org.uk/info/syndromes/electrical-status-epilepticus-during-slow-wave-sleep-esess all accessed April 2020

HOW DO I DO THIS?

Another huge challenge for me has been trying to navigate systems that seem to be full of "roadblocks".

What has your child taught you?

Lily has taught me that no matter what life/the fates throw your way there is always tomorrow.

How do you view your child's special needs?

My view of Lily's special needs is the tragedy of how difficult life is for her. She has worked so hard to gain skills only to have them slowly being eroded. However, she is happy and has a positive view of her self-worth.

What would you say to other parents of special needs children just beginning their journey? What advice/suggestions would you have for them?

No matter what diagnosis you are given today, your child is still the same person they were yesterday!! A diagnosis is just another fork in the road and, no matter how apparently devastating, you and your child will navigate it.

If you could think of one word to describe being a parent of a child with special needs what would it be?

Exhausting.

LILIAN AND MELISSA (AUSTRALIA)

Introduction:

My name is Lilian and I am the mother of three adult children: my eldest daughter is 58, my son is 51 and my youngest daughter Melissa is 47. I had another daughter who passed away after only two weeks. All my children, except my eldest daughter, were born prematurely: Melissa at least two (maybe three) months, and my other daughter who I lost was six weeks premature.

Melissa has been diagnosed with cerebral palsy.

We live in a regional city in Australia.

Was it always apparent to you that your child had special needs? If not, when did you notice that something was "different" about your child?

Melissa was about three or four months old when I took her to my doctor for a routine appointment. As soon as he saw her, he knew there was something very wrong and he referred her to a paediatrician. Melissa did not have normal cerebral palsy where she was unable to swallow—she ate normally, smiled, kicked her legs and she looked good in every way, except for a barely noticeable turn in one eye. However, she was not rolling over and so she underwent a brain scan which showed a big area of damage.

HOW DO I DO THIS?

If you have received a formal diagnosis for your child's special needs, when did this happen? Do you remember what feelings you experienced at the time and was the diagnosis a hard thing to come to terms with? Have you come to terms with it?

Melissa's formal diagnosis of cerebral palsy came when she was three to four months. I cannot remember what I felt; initially I was pretty much in a daze. Over the years it was hard to come to terms with, but I think I have now. Every now and again, when I hear about God doing amazing things in healing people, I still wish for her to recover. But overall, I think Melissa is okay about how she is and for her life to drastically change now might do more harm than good.

Did you research about how to help your child? What did you do? Which organisations/professionals did you reach out to?

Yes I got very interested in a program coming out of the US—the Philadelphia Institute for Human Potential[73] (now known as the Institutes for the Achievement of Human Potential) —and they seemed to be doing really amazing things with brain damaged children. We already had a busy schedule, but I began doing the patterning therapy (motor learning) which the Institute promoted as improving the "neurologic organisation" of brain damaged children. The patterning took up quite a lot of time and I did this with Melissa as best I could.

I reached out to speech and occupational therapists and Melissa had all the physiotherapy. I took Melissa to the Spastic Centre of NSW[74] in

---

[73] https://www.iahp.org accessed July 2020

[74] https://www.findandconnect.gov.au/ref/nsw/biogs/NE01579b.htm

AGE GROUP 30-50

Mosman Sydney (known since 2011 as the Cerebral Palsy Alliance[75]) because I had heard they were the best for treating brain damaged children. We would go down there about every six months and they helped me a lot more than my local doctors could. They were always happy that I shared the Institute's information with them, and everybody was on board with this. They used to write the program and I would take it down to Cootharinga[76] (a local support organisation) and they would follow it through too.

Melissa initially attended a school for children with special needs for a year and then from about Grade 3 she was able to go to a normal school where children with physical disabilities could attend. She did most of the things—apart from her physical limitations—that the other kids did.

What therapies did/do you use? What routines were/are helpful?

We did the brain patterning a couple of times a day at least. It generally took two people to do it and I must have done it when I had someone else to help me.

How has having a child with special needs affected your family? Your marriage? Your other children?

Our marriage was sort of rocky from day one. When Melissa was three, my husband left and later remarried. My eldest daughter went to live with him when she was 12. My son was 14 when he went to live with a

---

[75] https://cerebralpalsy.org.au/

[76] https://www.cootharinga.org.au/ all accessed July 2020

mate and by the time he was 15 he had a job and had left home permanently.

I may have been consumed with looking after Melissa and keeping her alive—doing whatever I had to do to make her life better—but I do not believe I did anything more than any other parent would do; my daughter had a need and I filled it.

I do not know how I survived it all. What was I thinking? Every day I put one foot in front of the other. To be honest, life seemed to be a blur, but in hindsight, I am happy with all the things I did, even if other people said I always seemed to be helping Melissa and not my other children. I do not have regrets. My other children had good lives and Melissa did not, and I just wanted her to have the best life she could have.

How do you take care of yourself? What self-care strategies do you use and how have you been able to implement them?

I do not think I totally neglected myself, but self-care was not high on my list of priorities. I was invited to join a squash group where I enjoyed playing squash and tennis with other mothers who had children with special needs.

Do you have a faith? If so, how has this helped you cope with life with your child?

It was Melissa who brought me back to having faith in the Lord. In the early days when my husband first left, I was invited to a healing meeting at a church. Melissa was having severe fits at that time and so I went, just for her to get healed. She was not healed at that time, but I decided to recommit my life to the Lord Jesus. As a little girl, I had been a Christian, but I had not attended church since I was a teenager (I was nearly 30 at the time) and had gone far away from God. When I went out to recommit my life to the Lord, God so touched my life that I was never the same. Suddenly, the world was a better place.

I was so sure that God was going to look after Melissa. I had not been sleeping because I was so anxious and worried that she would have a fit in the night and die. I was just able to trust God that she would be okay, which was the biggest thing for me, because she had been having the grand mal seizures[77]. Once I came back to the Lord, Melissa never had another fit in the night, even though for a time, she still had them during the day.

I guess the main thing for me was that I was able to think Melissa is not going to die, God is going to keep her alive. I used to go to healing services a lot and slowly Melissa just stopped taking the fits. After she was seven, she never did take another big fit like she had when she was younger. I put this down to faith in God and Him doing that, because this was beyond any human reasoning; all the doctors were so sure that Melissa would be on epilepsy medication all her life.

She astounded the doctors when she stopped taking the fits and she was able to get off the medication. Melissa learned to talk at a normal age. I home schooled her, and she learned to read very quickly. I put all of this down to the touch of God on her life. If ever there was anyone with a healing ministry—it did not matter to me what religion they were—we would be there, even if we had to drive for two hours. At the time, there was a charismatic renewal in the Catholic Church, and they had a lot of healing ministry. I would have Melissa prayed for. The one thing I

---

[77] https://www.mayoclinic.org/diseases-conditions/grand-mal-seizure/symptoms-causes/syc-20363458 accessed July 2020

always wanted for Melissa was for her to get out of the wheelchair and I often believed she would jump up and walk. Even when this did not happen, I knew God touched her in other ways.

How important/necessary is your family support or the support of your friends/networks? Do you feel as though you have enough support?

My parents were my best support; I could not have managed without them. My Mum was just a wonderful mother. I was on my own with my kids after my husband left and I used to go to my parents most weekends. I lived in a world totally consumed by looking after Melissa; I had no energy and nothing to give to anyone else; I did not want to be out partying or even to visit other people. I just spent all weekend with Mum and Dad until I became a born-again Christian, and then I made a whole new group of friends.

After my husband left and I had Melissa on my own, I withdrew from all my other friends. They tried to reach out to me, and I am sure they wanted to help me, but I just went into my shell, not wanting to be with anyone, especially people with 'normal' children. They all had normal, happy marriages and ordinary kids and I could not cope with any of that. I could not go over to my neighbours who had a little girl because I did not want to be with anyone whose life was so different to mine. My friends also stayed friends with my ex-husband and his new wife. I guess I felt sorry for myself. Without God, I could not handle it. So, I just walked away and lost them all.

This turned out to be good for me, because when I became a Christian and my life took a different turn, I needed friends who supported me because I would not have survived if I had not been surrounded by people who were praying for me and encouraging me and who would let me know that God could help me and heal Melissa. Some of this did not happen, but I just wanted to surround myself with these people like myself. I tended to stick with single Mums, and I made friends with ones who had gone through big traumas like I had. The first couple I was close to had lost their little girl through drowning and they came to know the Lord through that. They loved Melissa and they prayed for her and bought her gifts.

What do you hope/think the future holds for your child? Their living arrangements? A job? Marriage and children of their own?

I wanted Melissa to be a "normal" child and to grow into a "normal" adult. That was my dream and I felt I did everything in my power—as well as praying and asking God—for this to happen. But her life is not like this at all.

When Melissa first left school she went to a sheltered workshop (a workplace that provides a supportive environment where people with special needs can acquire job skills and vocational expertise) for about a year. She hated this and always wanted a normal job but, back then, this was not possible for people with special needs. When she was in her 20s, she wanted to go and live on her own and got supported accommodation with the Housing Commission. She became friendly with one of her neighbours who then became her partner. He is probably autistic and has lots of issues, but they have been together for about 20 years. The relationship between them is not good and is possibly a bit toxic, but she is happy that she has someone who loves her—and, in his own way, he does. He has his own place, but they are a couple and he receives a Carers Allowance to help her also. She always wanted children, but her partner did not, so they never had them, for which I am grateful.

HOW DO I DO THIS?

Even though Melissa is now 47 years old, I am still always aware of her needs. It is not like this with my other daughter; I think about Melissa every day and wonder how she is coping? Her personality now is very different to how she was as a little child; everyone loved her then but now it seems nobody does. She has a bitterness about her, and she puts people off. Now, with the NDIS, she has support workers, but if she did not have them, she would have no friends. They are good to Melissa but, in the past, she has had some who have not been so good.

Melissa has no reduced life expectancy because of the cerebral palsy, but because of things like sitting in the wheelchair, she has issues such as her kidneys not working properly. She has kidney stones, which the specialist said were a direct result of the drugs she was on. Melissa is also an asthmatic, but this is more of a by-product of her lifestyle and the drugs she has been on rather than because of the cerebral palsy. When she was little, she could have died from the seizures and as an adult she has been seriously ill with the kidney stones. There are things that do indicate that she may not live a long life. I do not know how I would handle it if she died before me, but I also hate the thought of dying and leaving her alone, but I have come to accept she is in God's hands, whatever happens.

I would like to think Melissa would live till she was 70 the same as others, but I would not want her to live the way she is living for another 20 years. She is still very dependent on me and this is a bit of a quandary. Because she is dependent on me, she has a sort of love/hate relationship with me. Melissa is angry at the life she has had to live because she, too, always wanted a normal life. She blames me because, in her mind, it is my fault the way things turned out. Indirectly, I guess it is, because the doctors and I thought she was due when in fact she was three months premature. We go from her love for me and needing me, to her asking why she did not just die that night. When she gets angry with life and has a bit of a meltdown, she takes it out on me, throwing things at me, and then calls the police to get me out of her house, saying I am abusing her.

So, the little girl who was so sweet, to the woman she has become, are quite different and I never thought she could change like that. That is extremely hard for me to come to grips with and yet I know life has made her like that: spending 47 years of life in a wheelchair and the things that have happened. Most of her dreams never came true. Melissa just sees it as all part of the fact that she has cerebral palsy. In a way, the fact that she has a good brain makes it harder for her.

What are/have been the joys of raising your child?

The main joy is that it drove me back to my faith because I possibly never would have done this without Melissa. I was happy in the life I lived, and we have shared some truly precious times, especially when she was a child and then a teenager, when the other children were out with friends and we were together at home.

What are/have been the hardest challenges raising your child?

The hardest challenge is seeing how my daughter is now, but the bottom line is "She is who she is, and I love her anyhow". The happy times are fewer and further apart, the older Melissa has gotten. We have become further and further apart as she has got older and she will often swear at me over the phone or hang up on me, which is something I never thought she could do. In my heart, I am still proud of her, and I tell her that sometimes, but I am about the only one who has that pride—all my friends just see the person Melissa has become, but I see through a mother's eyes, and I am proud of her. She has had to overcome a lot of disappointments and challenges. I believe God also is proud of her.

All my three children have had their issues and when I think about it, neither of my other children are who I dreamed they would be. I think it has a lot to do with life's challenges that they have had to face, also, being a part of a single parent family with a severely disabled sibling.

What has your child taught you?

I had no idea about what other parents with special needs children went through until I had Melissa. For example, I have a vague recollection that Cootharinga were having a stall and I was not even the least bit interested in supporting it. I have learned to be compassionate to other people and I have come back to the Lord. I have learned so much from having Melissa, just so much. I am a totally different woman to the young woman I was before I had her. Worlds apart, probably a hardhearted b#$&! who only cared about herself. Now, if I ever see a child in a wheelchair I want to cry and hug their mothers. If I hear about a situation, I say to God "Help me to help them". It has given me much compassion for others.

How do you view your child's special needs?

I do not take the attitude that it is a unique gifting or anything because I do not personally believe that the Almighty had that plan for Melissa's life. She is who she is, and she has a lot of difficulties to overcome, and they are always heavy on my heart. I would not say she has a great life.

I hear of people who have "normal" kids who are in their early 20s and the parents do not know where they are, and they do not talk to them. I hear about people who have not seen their children for 20 years and they are not allowed to see their own grandchildren. If you live long enough you hear about some of the things that some parents have had to cope with. My life has been almost "a walk in the park" compared to what some people have been through.

In the light of that, my life is okay. Even when she is in a bad mood, Melissa wants to ring me most days. I think I see her difficulties, but I accept she is who she is. I wish things were better, but it is okay; she has a couple of great carers, a mother who loves her, and a sister who also loves her, despite Melissa being nasty to her. And her partner, in his own way, loves her too. Some women have never had a boyfriend and have lived life on their own; Melissa has never known that. So, there is good and bad in it and she has a lot of things other people do not.

"Casting your cares on the Lord" (Psalm 55:22)[78] has been an ongoing process of learning for me. I put Melissa and her cares in a basket in my mind and I hold them up to the Lord and I say, "Lord, I give her to you" God reminded me about Moses' mother and I just had this real revelation that she probably cried all the tears that anyone could cry when she had to let go of her little son. She could do nothing more for this little baby, he was getting too big, so she put him in this basket and placed him in the river. She still got Miriam to keep an eye on him, but basically, she had to let go and she had to trust God that Moses had a destiny and that his life was important[79]. This has helped me. We all must come to that place, where we put our child in a basket and place them in a river and trust God. That is a new thing for me. Even though I have felt I have let go a million times from the time my daughter was little, this is a new letting go and I am freer than I have ever been.

---

[78] Psalm 55:22 Cast your cares on the LORD, and He will sustain you; He will never let the righteous be shaken (Holy Bible, NIV version © 2011-2019 Biblica).

[79] The story of Moses as a baby is told in the Holy Bible at Exodus 2:1-10

I live close to her and every time the ambulance goes past, I used to wonder if it was for Melissa and now, I do not even think about that. It is a new level of letting go and trusting God. I am 76 and maybe because I am getting old, God wants me to do that. The thought of leaving her was once unimaginable, but now I can think, you know what, she would be okay. Because I trust God.

What would you say to other parents of special needs children just beginning their journey? What advice/suggestions would you have for them?

I hope I would not be too negative because it is the hardest journey I have ever taken. I would not just say it is going to be okay, because it might not be. Most of the time I feel extremely sad when I know a family with a special needs child, but the last thing I would say is they do not know what is ahead of them because their journey may be different to mine.

With God I have hope, and so I would encourage them: "You can do it, God will help you, and there are some amazing things that can happen too". I press into God more than ever before and I need friends more than I thought I did. I never got close to people; I did not think I needed them and very few understood me and my situation. I would say now "First of all, you need God, then you need your friends and family."

When we went to the Uniting Church a few years ago, there was this little girl with a serious disability and my heart sank for her and her family. I could not be excited for them. I saw them recently and they remembered me as Melissa's mother. This little girl was now a teenager and she was quite happy and so were her parents and I thought, she is okay. Life has thrown them some challenges, but despite these, they have weathered the storm and come out happy.

If you could think of one word to describe being a parent of a child with special needs what would it be?

Resilience; inner strength.

Any final thoughts?

If you had asked me way back before Melissa was born would I want a child with special needs, I probably would have said no. But now, in this stage of my life, I am okay with it and I see it has made me into a much, much better person, with far more compassion for others than I had before Melissa.

HOW DO I DO THIS?

Please list any organisations in your country that you have found helpful.

- Cootharinga
  https://www.cootharinga.org.au

- Cerebral Palsy Alliance
  https://cerebralpalsy.org.au

- The National Disability Insurance Scheme (NDIS) has been a blessing. Even though it did not deliver exactly what we had hoped, it gave us much more than we ever had before.

- Overseas, the Philadelphia Institute for Human Potential (now known as the Institutes for the Achievement of Human Potential) at https://www.iahp.org

FAMILIES WITH MORE THAN ONE CHILD WITH SPECIAL NEEDS

- Zoe, Louise, 23 (auditory processing disorder), Harry, 12 (ADHD, autism, hearing loss and some dyslexia) and Tiger, 10 (ADHD, autism, anxiety), Australia

- Amy, Jeremy, Austin, 25, and Andrew, 19 (both Asperger's Syndrome), USA

- Ann, Jane, 45 (Down Syndrome) and Valen, 38 (epilepsy, autism, and Tourette's Syndrome), Australia

- April, Scott, Kellis, 21 (Asperger's Syndrome), Garrett, 20 (autism), Isaac, 19 (autism), Margaret, 16, Virginia, 14, Marianne, 10 (deafness), Rhetten, 8, April, 7 (deafness and autism) and Scott, 5, USA

ZOE, LOUISE, HARRY AND TIGER (AUSTRALIA)

Introduction:

My name is Zoe and I am a single Mum to Louise, 23, Harry, 12, and Tiger, who has just turned 10.

Louise has been diagnosed with auditory processing disorder; Harry has ADHD, autism, hearing loss and probably a touch of dyslexia; and Tiger has ADHD, autism, and anxiety.

We live in a regional city in Queensland, Australia.

Was it always apparent to you that your children had special needs? If not, when did you notice that something was "different" about your children?

Because I was a new Mum, it was hard for me to notice that Louise was "different". She had learning difficulties as a child—she had major struggles doing schoolwork, yet she could read or relay word-for-word verbatim from her "*Encyclopaedia of Animals*". She also had other issues—for example, refusing to wear certain types of clothing (or any clothing). Louise was a very curious child and loved the outdoors; she still does.

At different stages of her life, my daughter has had some social issues. It was not that she did not have friends—she would always have two or three—but socially she felt quite different from her friends. We moved

HOW DO I DO THIS?

from my hometown when Louise was about five or six, and she did much better socially.

She is still in touch with her best mate from childhood, who is married with two children. Louise is taking a different path and she has now finished university and is a qualified nurse. She was diagnosed with auditory processing disorder, where she hears three things at once. So, if I gave her an instruction to go downstairs and get a pair of scissors, she would miss certain words and get the wrong thing. Louise did her own research to see how she can better herself. Being a nurse and in a busy environment, listening to doctors' instructions and putting them into action means she must think carefully about what she is doing, if she is to make her job a success.

In this last year, her social life has improved; she is popular, has lost weight and has a really great group of friends. Louise is really loving life—apart from being a bit restrained with the COVID-19 pandemic—and has plans for her future. My daughter is like a success story for me. When she was little, she would walk on her toes. To correct this, she had to wear these special little boots, which brought her heels down. It was obvious Louise was wearing them and people would look at her strangely. I was a young Mum with Louise and I used to have these little boots on display, because when I looked at them, they gave me hope and a belief that things can get better. I have now put them away—the need to display them is now gone.

With Harry, in my stomach I felt like something was wrong. As soon as he was born, specialists came in and it was very apparent that something was not right. As time went on, it was more and more apparent there were things not bloody right. Harry was a floppy baby who was not meeting his milestones and he used to have convulsions or tremors. He was so unsettled, not sleeping, and unable to stand anything in his mouth like a dummy, and he did not eat food. I tried different programs for eating school and sleeping school but that did not help. Harry was just an exceedingly difficult baby.

As time went by, it became more obvious that something was not right with him. When he was six months old, I went to get his immunisations done and there was another mother there with her child getting theirs done at the same time. Harry was like a newborn baby laying in my arms while this other child was jumping around. Harry could not even hold his head up; he had no strength. I remember feeling sick and thinking, "This is just not right".

When he was eight months old, I met the same Mum and her baby at a shopping centre. Harry was unable to eat, but her baby literally gobbled up two tins of baby food. This really stuck out for me and I remember thinking there were so many things going on with my son and that something is seriously wrong.

We had visited medical paediatricians about all of Harry's issues and no-one would make any diagnosis. We looked up autism and went to Brisbane to get tests done because of his low muscle tone and they tried to look at all his different issues. There were lots of blood tests and so on.

With Tiger, he was perfect up until five or six months of age. His father and I had already separated, and one afternoon he took him for two hours. From that very first stay with his father, Tiger changed. He used to sleep, eat, and do everything right but after that day, he would shake his head in a funny way, and he was terrified, jumpy, and crying all the time. My beautiful peaceful little baby boy had just changed so much. It was all so disturbing. Because of Harry's issues I had a nurse and a psychologist who used to check in on us and they were genuinely concerned about the massive changes in Tiger and documented everything that was happening.

HOW DO I DO THIS?

If you have received a formal diagnosis for your children's special needs, when did this happen? Do you remember what feelings you experienced at the time and was the diagnosis a hard thing to come to terms with? Have you come to terms with it?

Harry's autism assessment was highly anticipated but, because there were so many things going on with him, it was hard to believe he would get the diagnosis he needed. I knew someone who knew about the assessment and they told me I *would* find out what was going on with my son. To me, there was no way that he was not autistic, and it was a relief when the assessment confirmed that he was. However, Harry was so well behaved doing the assessment that I also wondered how could this be so?

I had mixed emotions because I knew this was something we would have to carry for the rest of our lives. I was a bit sad, but I was more relieved that I was not going crazy. I had been made to feel this way because Harry was so young, and this was why the paediatrician and other professionals wanted to wait so long. In Australia, you need the paediatrician to sign off on a diagnosis so you can get the help you need. Because Harry had so many issues, I just did not want to have to wait. Even though I think there is also a stigma that comes with having a certain diagnosis, I just wanted to have some answers.

Tiger and Harry are chalk and cheese as far as behaviours go. They have totally different things happening. It was not a matter of Tiger copying a lot of things that Harry was doing. And because Harry was involved in so many therapies and stuff and we had the professionals coming to our home for this, they saw Tiger from when he was a newborn baby growing up—and they could see the changes and the concerning behaviours. And, Louise, my daughter, was doing her own research and she picked Tiger as being autistic. So, even though he and his brother were so totally different, I knew it was time for Tiger to also get assessed for autism. As it had been with Harry, it was a relief when he was diagnosed. I thought "Please let it be" because if Tiger was not autistic, his behaviour was really concerning—so, I sort of expected it for him. He has since been diagnosed with ADHD and suffers from anxiety.

He has also recently been reassessed for autism and diagnosed again.

Did you research about how to help your children? What did you do? Which organisations/professionals did you reach out to?

Some things I looked at online, but I was unable to do because of family. I really like occupational therapy and psychology. We did trial speech therapy and we need physiotherapy but it all costs money and we just cannot fit them all in. Tiger's speech is a nightmare and a couple of therapists we have had were dreadful, just absolute failures.

Our two GPs are husband and wife and we are very close with them.

We changed paediatricians and shopped around for a good one, and then went back to our original paediatrician, who, after initially making me feel like I was a crazy Mum, has a new respect for me these days. We don't use her as much now, but we have needed her to access other services.

What therapies did/do you use? What routines do you find helpful for your children?

We use psychology, occupational therapy and have gotten into some exercise classes. Sailing was something Tiger wanted to do, and he has become a different child—happier and confident. He has gone from

HOW DO I DO THIS?

having a violent meltdown six or seven times a day to once every two, three or four weeks, depending on what is happening. He has made so much progress and has accomplished so much in a short amount of time.

He used to be the child who had no friends and I can remember sitting with him and hugging him because all he wanted was just one friend. It was heartbreaking! But he never felt comfortable with other kids and school was very difficult as he was bullied by either teachers or students. My son could not look at people or talk to them and he was very reluctant to go out.

Now, because of his involvement with sailing, it has become much easier for Tiger to talk to others and it has been a great opportunity for socializing for both him and his brother. He has started getting friends of all ages—older, younger, and adults. He now has friends up and down the coast, in every sailing town from bloody Sydney to Cairns. Tiger has been to two national events and a family paid for him to compete in the NSW competition. He had been to a Nationals event in Brisbane and the conditions were extremely rough. The kid he was going to sail with got scared, so another child replaced him and sailed fantastically with Tiger. She asked him to sail with her down in Sydney in February just gone (2020). He came 37th out of 70, the youngest child in his division, in the absolute top of the range at the national event. In his age group in Queensland he would probably be one of the best sailors, but they do not go by age. Tiger has lots of issues—he did not know where the start line was, and he did not tell us this until the last night.

Harry is just a screen kid; we home-school him and so we access some home-school groups, but they are all closed now during this COVID-19 pandemic. Harry's learning disabilities were diagnosed, and our

FAMILIES WITH MORE THAN ONE CHILD WITH SPECIAL NEEDS

education system didn't suit his needs. He is doing much better than Tiger being home-schooled and is progressing.

We normally have a good routine doing sailing a couple of times a week, home-school and therapies. Because of the pandemic quarantining, therapies are going online so it is a little bit of sameness for the boys.

How has having children with special needs affected your family?

Now the boys are a little older it is easier, but in the early days it was difficult. I lost a lot of friends. I remember being at Mum's and a friend from school came out to visit. Harry was a headbanger and he started headbanging in front of her. I tried to explain what was happening, but I never saw her again. This is the normal for me.

In the earlier days it was all about family life and I had support, but it was still difficult. My sister had two little boys about the same age as Harry and Tiger and they were just so different. It made things hard. My sister is more understanding these days and she and the boys go do fun things together.

I had to plan and get the kids prepared for everything—for example, we were not able to just go to the movies with people. And it still takes a lot of planning to do something like this and usually we have to walk out at least once. We go on sailing trips and where others take only three hours, we need six hours to get to our destination.

Things like not being able to go to a nice restaurant are hard.

Things are a little bit easier now and we can be more flexible than we used to be, but still there is a lot going on. I s#!* myself thinking about what could happen. Lots of small changes can affect the kids in a big way—for example: moving a table the other way; having a green light instead of a red one at the traffic lights; or not having the right park at the shopping centre. We used to like going to the markets and local things and it used to be too hard to do that, but now things like that have become more manageable.

I broke up with the boys' Dad early, and, in the early days, he was an a*hole. For example, when he knew that I wanted to home-school the boys it gave him more ammunition to use against me. He just had no consideration of the effects that mainstream schooling was having on them. We both had a meeting with the school, who had done everything to prepare Harry to go from Year 3 to 4—same teacher, same kids, same classroom—and the Principal, the teacher, the psychologist and the OT were all there. The school said what had happened here and went over it all, but he was still unsupportive and not understanding of the situation at all. Even when I did pull the kids out, he threatened to take me to court to get them put them back in. He has moved on now, but he is also seeing the fact that the boys are going places and are happier.

How do you take care of yourself? What self-care strategies do you use and how have you been able to implement them?

I smoke a lot of cigarettes and I drink lots and lots of cups of tea.

I do not have many interests but in this past week I am feeling accomplished as I have learned to make kombucha and I have started a garden. There is also a little art thing I am wanting to do.

I also read the Bible and I like to look at things about the Bible on You Tube.

I am also heavily involved with the sailing and I have some responsibilities there.

Do you have a faith? If so, how has this helped you cope with life with your child?

I believe in God and Jesus as our Saviour. I believe that the kids' illnesses are demonic and something that has been brought on by the medicines that we have taken, the vaccines and the air we breathe. This world is not the way it is supposed to be, and I do not believe these illnesses are a naturally occurring thing. I believe they are a bioweapon that we must pray against.

It makes me sad to think my kids are not at their full potential, but then I do not know that for sure. Maybe they are supposed to be that way? They can focus on things and they have a vast knowledge of their interests. It is obsessive but it makes them happy. A lot of people never find happiness.

I am grateful to God and I just hope that I am doing the right thing.

How important/necessary is your family support or the support of your friends/networks? Do you feel as though you have enough support?

I am not sure about this. My Mum used to come down and help out a lot, but she is not very healthy and now she is not able to take the kids to places like the park. I think you get to a point where you think "This is it" regarding support. I have a couple of dear friends who come around once a term.

HOW DO I DO THIS?

I am at the stage where I am handling it on my own and I just think "This is life".

What do you hope/think the future holds for your children? Their living arrangements? A job? Marriage and children of their own?

I would think that Tiger would be fine to one day go out and find his own home, go to University, and get a job—so long as he can control his thoughts and his temper. His thought processes wear him (and everyone around him) out when he cannot do something. The ADHD and his anxiety make his thought processes difficult and, if he could change this, he would be a highly successful person.

Tiger can make a sandwich and things like that and Harry is starting to get to that stage. If he finds his niche, he will be so successful. He is talking about getting a job once he turns 14. His dream job would be working at EB Games but, by law, he must be 18 to work there. I think Harry will need a lot more help as an adult and I do worry more about him being out on his own.

Harry also wants to have kids one day, but Tiger has not really thought about this. Tiger will go and do things around the house whereas Harry is lazier and is happier to just sit on his computer.

I think the boys do have the potential to go out on their own, although it is quite possible that when the boys are 30, they still might be living with me.

What are/have been the joys of raising your children?

They are just unique and themselves. They are my kids—take the autism out and they are still my kids. They have funny ideas and ways that no-one would understand but me.

They are beautiful.

What are/have been the hardest challenges raising your children?

I would say their Dad and home-schooling.

When the boys were really young it was so difficult, but this was also because I did not understand what was upsetting them. Even to this day, I sometimes think "What the hell has happened now?"

There are different difficulties now. For example, Tiger is extremely strong and can be very violent and that is so hard; when your own child is bashing s#!* out of you. Or Harry will hurt himself when he is really angry and that is extremely hard to see.

What have your children taught you?

My children have taught me how to be their advocate. Over the years, I have had many, many, many fights with specialists and doctors, advocating for all three of my children not to be medicated; I have literally begged for this not to happen. There have been constant fights to get tests I wanted done. For example, a few years back Tiger had blood in his poo. One doctor told me it was all fine but then our regular doctor said "No, it's not".

HOW DO I DO THIS?

My children have taught me to have the balls to keep going when I have known that something is not right. It was so hard when the boys were being bullied at school, especially in the playground, and I would have to talk to the teachers every morning and every afternoon. It is not fair for kids to be bullied; for them it is now a nightmare to go to playgrounds.

How do you view your children's special needs?

A bit of a mixture of being difficult and being what makes them unique.

What would you say to other parents of special needs children just beginning their journey? What advice/suggestions would you have for them?

Hang in there! It is gonna be a rough and bumpy road where everything is uncertain. Some days are fine, you think you are making progress—and then the next day, for no reason you can understand, all the progress is gone, and you have to start again.

I would say "Just friggen breathe".

If you could think of one word to describe being a parent of a child with special needs what would it be?

Exhausting.

Any final thoughts?

For me there is lots of uncertainty about the future. It is scary, because as kids I can protect them to a certain extent, but once they are adults and in the workforce, there is nothing I can do.

Now, with the COVID-19 pandemic, parents are on Facebook complaining about home-schooling. I think "Are you serious?" Some people will never understand. I have a giggle because and I think "Whatever".

Please list any organisations in your country that you have found helpful.

- Australian Sailing – https://www.sailing.org.au/qld

- Advocacy – https://independentadvocacy.org.au/services
  Around two or three years ago I did have trouble with the NDIS (National Disability Insurance Scheme) and we had advocacy, who were amazing. In the end, I'd had enough of it all, but they pushed me and they supported me and that was something huge for me. In the end, we won above what we expected to win.

- Psychology – Having that support was like having a friend, when there was nobody else, for understanding our family life.

ANN, JANE AND VALEN (AUSTRALIA)

Introduction:

Hi, my name is Ann Greer and I have three adult children—two daughters and a son. My elder daughter Jane and my son Valen have significant disabilities. I live in Townsville, in North Queensland, Australia—as does Valen—and Jane lives in Bundaberg with her husband. All three of my children are grown adults and living their best lives—and this is something that makes me feel very blessed.

Was it always apparent to you that your children had special needs? If not, when did you notice that something was "different" about your children?

Jane is 45, born with Down Syndrome[80] and diagnosed at five days. My mother, a midwife, recognised this immediately but did not say anything to us.

My son Valen is 38 and our youngest, and he was diagnosed with uncontrolled epilepsy at 18 months, with autism at around three and with Tourette's Syndrome[81] at 15.

---

[80] https://www.betterhealth.vic.gov.au/health/conditionsandtreatments/down-syndrome

[81] https://tourette.org.au/about-tsaa/what-is-tourette-syndrome/ accessed June 2020

FAMILIES WITH MORE THAN ONE CHILD WITH SPECIAL NEEDS

If you have received a formal diagnosis for your children's special needs, when did this happen? Do you remember what feelings you experienced at the time and was the diagnosis a hard thing to come to terms with? Have you come to terms with it?

When Jane was born, I was devastated for a short while, but I soon realised she was more "Jane" than she was Down Syndrome. We just started treating her like any other baby. I think it was a great advantage that she was the eldest and we had no real way of knowing what she should or could be doing.

Valen was a different story. I was already reeling from how he was operating in the world—constantly crying, roaming around, hurting the other children, not talking and not sleeping—and I was shocked to discover that I had a second child with a disability. It took a little longer to find the point where I could accept that "this" was happening to me again. Later, I started to understand that "this" was not something happening to me at all but was actually Valen's journey.

Did you research about how to help your children? What did you do? Which organisations/professionals did you reach out to?

When Jane was quite young—under five—I worked out that really lovely people can give you some really terrible advice. I reached out to other parents—many of whom were much older than me. We met regularly at an early intervention group and I found them to be a wonderful emotional and information resource.

When Valen came along 38 years ago, most professionals did not really understand autism. So, I read books by people with autism and reached out to a few people who truly supported me and us as a family.

HOW DO I DO THIS?

What therapies did/do you use?

When my children were small, there was little therapy available. I did not trust many therapists but the ones that I did trust were a wonderful support.

How has having children with special needs affected your family? Your marriage? Your other children?

My marriage foundered but the relationship with the children's Dad has stayed strong. He is part of our family and I have tremendous respect for his support and love for his children.

I think having two siblings who had disabilities probably did affect my middle daughter. She is a highly successful specialist doctor and in a wonderful marriage with two great sons. I think that she was adversely affected but she was able to use that experience to become a remarkable person in her own right.

How do you take care of yourself? What self-care strategies do you use and how have you been able to implement them?

I worked out—albeit a bit late—that I was separate to all my children. I stopped trying to live my life through their successes or failures and chose to provide a life for each of us where we flourished rather than survived or drowned. There were months, years and possibly at least one decade where I could not achieve flourishing, but the aspiration remained strong.

I now live alone and see my children regularly. I am proud of Jane's level of independence. She is now married and lives in another town and is a remarkable woman. It has taken me a long time to be more caring of myself; I have moved from being a "rescuer" in my early life to being extremely careful to be caring without being enabling.

Do you have a faith? If so, how has this helped you cope with life with your child?

I started out life as a Catholic but am now totally lapsed. I do not believe in religion, but I have a strong belief in God, and I get enormous strength from that.

How important/necessary is your family support or the support of your friends/networks? Do you feel as though you have enough support?

My mother was a saint and she was supportive of me, as her daughter, and of my family. It was not a perfect relationship, but she was the person that I could rely on the most.

The children's father and I broke up when our son was two years old. He remains supportive and has always been there—particularly for Valen.

In the early times with the children, I often felt very alone and that no-one stepped up to help.

What do you hope/think the future holds for your children? Their living arrangements? A job? Marriage and children of their own?

Some of this is already achieved for Jane. She will not have children, but she is incredibly happy to be a married woman.

Val now has full support. He had been living with his Dad, who moved out, and Valen stayed on in the house with support from a team. I see this as the first opportunity that he has had to live a life of his own and I am so excited for him!

I do not spend much time ruminating on the future as I think it is best to stay firmly in the present. I do, however, feel very hopeful that my children have lives that are, and will continue to be, very good.

What are/have been the joys of raising your children?

I am not naturally drawn to motherhood, but I know that I have been a good mother. I have taught my children to be as independent as they are able to be, and I have never projected my own ambitions onto them—I feel enormously proud of that.

What are/have been the hardest challenges raising your children?

There were a lot of hard things but truthfully, I cannot really bring them to mind now. I know that it is still hard to see Valen in a seizure.

I can honestly say that I spend no time feeling sad for what might have been.

FAMILIES WITH MORE THAN ONE CHILD WITH SPECIAL NEEDS

What have your children taught you?

I have learned so much from all three of my children. As a result of being their parent, I have learned to be patient, I know who I am and what I am capable of. I have been able to develop a career in disability because of my children.

I now have a wonderful life of my own and I count my blessings every day.

How do you view your children's special needs?

I love and accept all my children for who they are, and I am enormously proud of all of them. I do not love any one of them more than another.

What would you say to other parents of special needs children just beginning their journey? What advice/suggestions would you have for them?

See your child as a child first and the disability as a secondary aspect of him or her. This is not the same as not accepting the disability; it is more about what you focus on.

Try hard to give your child ordinary experiences, to take risks and to have high expectations. It will not be the level of disability that will stop him or her from having a good life—it will be the crushing lack of expectation experienced by many people with disabilities.

HOW DO I DO THIS?

If you could think of one word to describe being a parent of a child with special needs what would it be?

Two words—full-on and unrelenting. Maybe more—driven by love.

APRIL, SCOTT, KELLIS, GARRETT, ISAAC, MARGARET, VIRGINIA, MARIANNE, RHETTEN, APRIL AND SCOTT (USA)

Introduction:

My name is April Tribe Giauque (pronounced Juke). I am married to my second husband, Scott, and I am the mother of a small nation of nine. To answer the next question—yes, I gave birth to all of them. My eldest five were with my first husband but we were divorced after nine years of him struggling with drugs, alcohol, mental illness, and abuse. I then married Scott. He took all five children on as his own, and we had four more children together. I share all of this in my book *Pinpoints of Light: Escaping the Abyss of Abuse*[82].

Kellis is 21 and has Asperger's Syndrome. I am proud of his determination. He now lives on his own and works full-time as head lifeguard and a top swim instructor. Kellis is trying to save to go to college. He enjoys hanging out with his best friend Drew and his cousins. He loves routine and is now dating. ☺

Garrett is 20; he has autism and is an artist. He is designing a movie of all his favorite characters which range from Pokémon to all the Author characters from public television. He draws twelve cells per day—first in black and white and then in full color.

He works at home and will live with us for the rest of his life due to the escalation of his mental health challenges. He only has our family, but he

---

[82] Available at: http://www.amazon.com/dp/B07SH2ZZWT

HOW DO I DO THIS?

is content and filled with love. He is close to Jesus and shares that he knows how to draw so well and understands animals because he saw Jesus create the world while he was in Heaven. I smile deeply at this. Garrett knows our Heavenly Father, and is an angel living among us. He knows his creation is important and has such kindness.

Isaac is 19 and he also has autism. He is my stuntman, a high sensory-seeking young man who loves jumping off the roof onto the trampoline. He lives with my parents as a steppingstone towards his independence, paying them a small rent and helping them with household chores. Isaac also works part-time at UPS and he never misses work. He has gained one friend. Isaac can play tough and stubborn on the outside—all as a protection—but on the inside, he has a heart that is tender and sweet. He shows it to my Mom and that makes me smile deeply. I am proud of him working on his independence and finding a friend.

Margaret Susanna is 16 and she is my singer, songwriter, artist, and free spirit. Her gift is that she can see anything and duplicate it visually with a curvy flair. Faces and portraits are her specialty. School is not really her thing and she just endures the academics of it, but loves choir, cosmetology school, and any kind of social connections.

Virginia Grace is 14 and knows her life plan. She is studying to be an obstetrician/gynecologist; women and babies are her "thing." She has a best friend and they are inseparable. School is critical to her and she needs constant reminding of how proud we are of her and her accomplishments. I do my best to use words of affirmation and show her that she is loved and important. Virginia has an organized creative side to her that is fun to watch come out. I love her drive and determination to make a different life for herself.

Marianne Ellen is 10 and she is deaf. Nearly everyone knows American Sign Language and signs with her. Marianne is a swimmer and an artist. She is powerful in her determination and has always reminded me of a lion filled with power, strength, and stubbornness, who needs her pride/tribe close to her. Marianne writes stories and illustrates them; she keeps asking when I am going to make her work into a book (I had better get onto that!).

Rhetten Scott is 8. He is a Lego master and top reader. Rhetten loves to be a big brother and has a heart on the pulse of the family, communicating with his sisters through his fluency in ASL. He helps many in the family as the interpreter for his sisters. He is also an empath and yet delivers love through his humour; he is so funny! Rhetten loves his routine and always has his shoes and backpack ready for school.

April Rose is nearly 7. She is deaf and has autism. She was born on my birthday, April 28th, so I had to give her my name. Her arrival and the challenges of her autism and deafness were the catalyst in our cross-country 1300-mile move from Utah to Texas. We simply needed better schooling to help her with her double challenge. I knew how to do the autism part, but I knew I needed more supports with her being deaf as well.

April is filled with energy and has sixth-sense types of powers (she is like a cat and can escape harm). She loves art, rainbows, unicorns, gum, and peanut butter and jelly sandwiches. She has two guardian angels named Ethel and Hazel who watch over her. She can still escape at night (at 1 or 2 a.m.) if she cannot sleep and will scooter around the neighborhood. And yes, we have incredible neighbors. She is improving—and we are all getting some rest.

Scott Joseph is our baby. He is 5, loves math, reading, playing with his trains and cars. As being the youngest in a nation of people, his vocabulary is surprisingly huge, and he will say the funniest things. He is our spot of sunshine and light. He reminds all that God loves them, that Jesus is his best friend, and he will be found singing *"I am a Child of God"* to his trains and cars as he plays.

HOW DO I DO THIS?

Was it always apparent to you that your children had special needs? If not, when did you notice that something was "different" about your children?

Garrett (20) was around eight months old when I knew something was different—but I had no idea what. I remember his lack of babbling and that he would not reach out towards toys. When he was 18 months old, the tantrums, self-injurious behaviors, and lack of walking were getting me worried. I was married to my first husband at that time and my family life was not stable. We did the best we could, but at age three Garrett was diagnosed with autism.

If you have received a formal diagnosis for your children's special needs, when did this happen? Do you remember what feelings you experienced at the time and was the diagnosis a hard thing to come to terms with? Have you come to terms with it?

For our family, the diagnosis was an interesting event. My focus had been on Garrett and not on anyone else in the family. In six years, I had four children. Our pediatrician gave us information about a research project where the genetic components of autism were being studied. He said that they did diagnostic testing for *free* and would follow up for the next four years.

I jumped at the opportunity. The catch was the whole family had to be involved. I signed up all the children (except Margaret; she was only five months old at the time).

They did all the blood work on everyone (me, my husband, Kellis, Garrett, and Isaac) and it was a week's worth of daily testing, observations, and MRIs. Bottomline was that, following the week, I was handed the diagnosis on four people: Kellis (Asperger's Syndrome),

FAMILIES WITH MORE THAN ONE CHILD WITH SPECIAL NEEDS

Garrett (low-functioning autism), Isaac (PDD-NOS[83]), and my first husband with possible bi-polar/schizophrenia.

This was a devastating week. I remember holding onto the stack of papers and slowly going over the words again and again until the pages slipped from my hands, carpeting the floor with the words I could no longer read.

Five months later, as if right on cue, Margaret started showing signs of regression, and developmental delays. I felt my world spinning and crash. To cope with all of this and his mental health issues, my husband turned to street drugs, porn, and alcohol. Then if we were too much, we would feel his wrath physically against us.

Did you research about how to help your children? What did you do? Which organizations/professionals did you reach out to?

Upon receiving all the diagnoses, I was recommended to the Northern Utah Autism Program. This program was funded by Health and Human Service monies. That is significant because it was not educational dollars and it meant that they could require parents to volunteer at least 40 hours a month in the classroom for your child to stay in the program.

Garrett and Isaac both went through the program (Kellis was too old). I was taught and trained in ABA (Applied Behavior Analysis), DTT (Discrete Trial Training)[84] and Play Therapy. This program changed my

---

[83] https://www.healthline.com/health/autism/pdd-nos accessed July 2020

[84] DTT is a practitioner-led, structured instructional procedure that breaks tasks down into simple subunits to shape new skills. Often employed up to **6–7 hours per day** for children with autism, the technique relies on the use of prompts, modeling, and positive reinforcement strategies to facilitate the child's learning.

life, allowing for a new routine and normalcy to enter our home—despite the chaos my first husband was creating.

What therapies did/do you use? What routines do you find helpful for your child?

We did occupational, speech and play therapies, and then school five days a week for six hours a day. I had—and still have—visual schedules, task breakdowns, and practice DTT for my sons and daughter. I still do occupational and play therapies with them. The program lasted for 2.3 years for us. We were getting a handle on things.

How has having children with special needs affected your family? Your marriage? Your other children?

This question is too big. The effects of having children with special needs added a lot of stress to my first marriage. My first husband and I divorced because he was too dangerous; he had threatened to kill one of my children because of their challenging behaviours. Healing is still ongoing. My older daughters work with therapists to help them cope with abandonment and anger issues about their biological father's challenges.

My second marriage is stable but step-parenting to all the special needs in our family is a challenge. Further challenges have been added with two more deaf children, a cross-country move, and my second husband's health crisis and unemployment for four years. But if there is one thing that my Heavenly Father blessed me with it is drive; the drive to never settle, but find answers to challenges.

How do you take care of yourself? What self-care strategies do you use and how have you been able to implement them?

Self-care is simple: prayer, Scriptures, walks in nature, pondering, music that I feel Him with, living the Word of Wisdom. I only drink water, I abstain from tea, coffee, alcohol, tobacco, or drugs; I eat plants (vegetables and some fruit) first, then moderation in meat/dairy, and light on the bread. And finally, I write—to save my sanity and express my stories.

Do you have a faith? If so, how has this helped you cope with life with your children?

I am a member of the Church of Jesus Christ of Latter-Day Saints. I am the daughter of my Heavenly Father. I am a covenant-keeping woman. I know my value, my worth, my gifts, my strengths, and that everything comes from Him. He has taken my weaknesses, and through Jesus Christ, they have become my strengths. I fully rely on Him for my every breath to allow it all to work.

All I have ever wanted was my large family to individually know their Heavenly Father and Jesus Christ through the power and confirmation of the Holy Spirit. This prayer of mine never ceases.

I know that there is time for all to come to know Him. I pray, teach faith in the home, and do my best to love them the way God does. Some children have wandered and my first spouse left it all behind, but I cling to a ray of hope and light that God has given me—that He knows His Family Tree and that He can mend the broken branches of that Tree. I must trust that.

HOW DO I DO THIS?

How important/necessary is your family support or the support of your friends/networks? Do you feel as though you have enough support?

Great question. I have had to work on building relationships and a network of friends. Trusting others has not been easy and many have abandoned relationships when they understand the depth of my life. I have only ever relied on Heavenly Father, but since I was 39, I started to realize that I needed friends.

God has helped me understand the art of friendship through the scriptures and that if I am focused on serving others then light and healing happens. It is not about me; it is about them.

What do you hope/think the future holds for your children? Their living arrangements? A job? Marriage and children of their own?

The futures for all my children are so different, but I know that they will be as independent as possible and that I am blessed with gifts and talents to help them get to where they need to be. I hope for many to get married, for grandchildren, and for them to know God loves them. I pray that they find work that is engaging and meaningful, and that, every night as they rest their head, they know that God loves them.

What are/have been the joys of raising your children?

The joy has been watching them discover their gifts and talents.

FAMILIES WITH MORE THAN ONE CHILD WITH SPECIAL NEEDS

What are/have been the hardest challenges raising your children?

Watching their pain, their struggle, and standing to the side allowing them to struggle and not rush in to fix their problems. Learning how to let go and let God.

What have your children taught you?

Advocacy, patience, and most importantly, what love is—that it can fill your soul like a beautiful Christmas, or be as painful as being lost in the darkest cave, but that there is always hope of a new hour/day to ask for forgiveness and try again.

How do you view your children's special needs?

I view these as a gift that they are blessed with—to help me and all those they come in contact with, to become a better person.

What would you say to other parents of special needs children just beginning their journey? What advice/suggestions would you have for them?

Stay strong in your faith and LOVE them for THEM. Do not look for fixes or cures and do not start the blaming "witch hunt" —it is destructive and will separate you from the moments you have with your children.

HOW DO I DO THIS?

Find therapies, find ways to accept them, yet set expectations for them. Do love, snap pictures, and keep a "Thankful Journal" daily and you will see the changes over time.

Remember that time is a gift and a blessing. As I think back to my children doing self-injurious behaviors, I thought that that would be my full life, but really, things change with time.

If you could think of one word to describe being a parent of a child with special needs what would it be?

LOVE

Any final thoughts?

FAMILIES WITH MORE THAN ONE CHILD WITH SPECIAL NEEDS

Please list any organizations in your country that you have found helpful.

- Northern Utah Autism Program:
  www.nuaparents.com

- Spectrum Academy Charter School (I am a founding parent of this school)
  https://www.spectrumcharter.org

- Texas School for the Deaf
  https://www.tsd.state.tx.us

AMY, JEREMY, AUSTIN AND ANDREW (USA)

Introduction:

We are a family located in Grand Blanc, Michigan, USA. I'm Amy, the mother to Austin (25) and Andrew (19) and wife to Jeremy (stepdad). Austin and Andrew are both diagnosed with Asperger's Syndrome on the autism spectrum.

FAMILIES WITH MORE THAN ONE CHILD WITH SPECIAL NEEDS

Was it always apparent to you that your children had special needs? If not, when did you notice that something was "different" about your children?

I was raised around all girls and had all female cousins. My son was the first boy in our family, so I really had no idea what "typical" behaviour was. Austin was always a bit more active and went from thing to thing and, right from the start, he was very inquisitive and intelligent. When we visited the doctors over the first 5-6 years, I was told he was a "typical" boy. At my grandfather's funeral an aunt approached me and said, "You know Asperger's runs in the family, so keep that in the back of your mind", to which my reply was "Well, the doctor thinks he's normal".

If you have received a formal diagnosis for your children's special needs, when did this happen? Do you remember what feelings you experienced at the time and was the diagnosis a hard thing to come to terms with? Have you come to terms with it?

When Austin was six years old, we were told that he was ADHD[85] from a neurologist and doctor. At the age of 12, a teacher in sixth grade slid me some information—with a title of "Asperger's Syndrome"[86] — during parent teacher conferences. I picked it up and the teacher said, "I think your son has this. Please ask the school to test him." I was speechless! Afterwards, as I read it in my car, I laughed, and I cried.

---

[85] https://www.adhdaustralia.org.au/about-adhd/what-is-attention-deficit-hyperactivity-disorder-adhd

[86] https://www.webmd.com/brain/autism/mental-health-aspergers-syndrome

HOW DO I DO THIS?

When I got home, I had Austin sit down with me and asked him to read the paper. Then he started saying "Mom, that's me! I have Asperger's!" It was a huge light bulb moment for us—and we laughed and cried together. I then wrote a letter to the school requesting an evaluation. They came back about a month later with the diagnosis. We developed an IEP[87] (Individual Education Plan) and then went back to our doctor and handed him the same paper and said, "We think Austin has this." His response was "What is Asperger's?" That was the last time we took our children there.

A month later, at Andrew's classroom, we discussed the diagnosis for Austin. We asked his teacher to keep her mind open and to please let me know if she noticed anything with Andrew. A month later, she called me and said "I see a lot of the signs. We should have a formal evaluation". So, at six years of age, Andrew was diagnosed as well.

It took me a lot to process the information. I was in a new relationship/marriage. We had to learn a new "normal".

Did you research about how to help your children? What did you do? Which organisations/professionals did you reach out to?

I reached out to the local autism support group and jumped right in. We attended monthly support group meetings. I started a monthly Asperger's social group for teens with Asperger's and their families, which quickly took off. After a few years, I joined the Board of Directors. We then founded and opened the area's first Autism Support and Resource Center. Through the Autism Center we held support

---

[87] https://www.understood.org/en/school-learning/special-services/ieps/what-is-an-iep all accessed July 2020

group meetings, monthly socials for different age groups, sensory room, special summer camp and sports.

What therapies did/do you use? What routines do you find helpful for your children?

Following a visual schedule worked the best for us. We color-coded everything in life from school classwork to home. We used a positive behaviour plan and reward system. Andrew used occupational therapy at school and home which proved successful for him.

How has having children with special needs affected your family? Your marriage? Your other children, if you have them?

Our marriage eventually failed. At the time, we were a blended family of six. I had two boys, and he also had two children. There was a lot of jealousy from the stepchildren because of the amount of attention that my children required.

Our family was in denial for a while, until I was able to sit down and go over things line by line with them. They have been supportive and caring.

How do you take care of yourself? What self-care strategies do you use and how have you been able to implement them?

We found out about respite and I would take one night a week out for me. Now that the boys are older, I travel. That is how I self-care, I get out of the life situation and focus on me. It is so important to take care of yourself.

Do you have a faith? If so, how has this helped you cope with life with your children?

Absolutely, I have always believed God would not give me more than I can handle. I questioned this numerous times, but we have overcome a lot.

How important/necessary is your family support or the support of your friends/networks? Do you feel as though you have enough support?

Support from family and friends is huge. They were able to be there to watch the boys when I needed to just get out of the situation. They offered a break for a weekend when I was overloaded, and someone to vent to without fear of judgement.

What do you hope/think the future holds for your children? Their living arrangements? A job? Marriage and children of their own?

My boys still live at home at 19 and 25. I am looking into buying them a house for the future and they will more than likely live together forever. Even though they are six years apart, they are best friends and do most things together. I see one working part-time, as he does now, and the other eventually getting back into full time work as a Mechanical Engineer. He has the brains for it but very poor executive functioning processes.

FAMILIES WITH MORE THAN ONE CHILD WITH SPECIAL NEEDS

What are/have been the joys of raising your children?

It has been wonderful seeing them flourish when given the tools they needed to be successful in school and life.

What are/have been the hardest challenges raising your children?

It has been a challenge to remind myself that, as long as they are happy, then that has to be good enough for me. What I want for them and what they want for themselves can often be two different things.

What have your children taught you?

I never took on an advocate role until my sons were diagnosed. We started to pave the way in our town for kids with Asperger's/autism. Together, the parents of our Center supported each other. We worked with schools to help our children to flourish and succeed in the school setting. Many teachers fought the disability and I had to learn to teach the teachers to understand from a different perspective.

How do you view your children's special needs?

The different ability is something to be embraced and worked with and is what makes them unique. Although this is not always easy, I would not change it.

HOW DO I DO THIS?

What would you say to other parents of special needs children just beginning their journey? What advice/suggestions would you have for them?

Stay strong and stay focused because you have a lifelong journey ahead of you. Reach out for help—do not be afraid to ask! Join as many support groups as you can and if there is not one local to you, START ONE!

Never be afraid to speak up. If it doesn't feel right, it probably isn't.

If you could think of one word to describe being a parent of a child with special needs what would it be?

Tiring.

Please list any organisations in your country that you have found helpful.

- Autism Support and Resource Center, serving Genesee County and: neighbouring communities: at https://www.geneseeautism.org

CONCLUSION

It is no easy task to bare your soul and answer questions—which, by their very nature—can be emotional, thought provoking and invasive.

It is no easy task to even find the space to do this when your children are demanding of so much of your time and energy.

In compiling these interviews, I was mindful that I was asking these parents to allow others to enter their own personal world, even though it was for just a little while. Each of these incredible parents approached the task of telling their story from the space of wanting to help others on a similar journey. I could see myself, and my own story, in every single one of these parents. We all come from different countries, have different nationalities and backgrounds and our children are at all different ages, but we are bound by a common thread. When you meet another special needs parent, you know that they know. They *get it*.

Now that you have read this book, it is my hope that you have received encouragement, practical tools, information, and resources that you may not have considered. It is my hope that you realise that you are not alone, and there are others who have journeyed right where you are now, and who can meet you right where you are at.

The road is long and undeniably filled with potholes and roadblocks, but there are also smooth stretches of highway here and there. Now that my daughter is an adult, I can see how our journey has been an incredible one, and I feel excitement for what lies ahead. I would never swap my experience of being Sarah's Mum. As time passes and she continues to grow into her potential, I am more and more thankful for who she is.

HOW DO I DO THIS?

We got through the hard yards and I believe you will too.

All the parents in this book know how hard this journey can be. If you are a parent experiencing isolation and burnout, please know that you are not alone. Reach out to someone who can help. This could be a social worker, a friend, a family member, a teacher, a therapist, your church (and God!) if you are a person of faith, a counsellor, or a phone consultation through a service such as Lifeline. Join Facebook groups (just type "special needs groups" into the search area) and network with other parents in this way, as well as face-to-face.

For reference, I am including some mental health resources:

- **Australia:** The Top 30 Mental Health Organisations in **Australia** are at https://my.salvos.org.au/toolkit/resource/top-30-mental-health-organisations-in-australia/834/

- **USA:** The Top 20 mental health organisations in **USA** http://davidsusman.com/2016/07/07/top-20-us-mental-health-organizations-part-1/ and http://davidsusman.com/2016/07/14/top-20-us-mental-health-organizations-part-2/

- **United Kingdom:** https://www.nhs.uk/conditions/stress-anxiety-depression/mental-health-helplines/ and https://www.mentalhealth.org.uk/

Please feel free to reach out to me by email at meredith@meredithswift.org about anything that I have touched on in this book.

May God bless you all.

MY BOOKS ARE ALL AVAILABLE ON AMAZON OR DIRECT FROM ME

My website and blog is at https://www.meredithswift.org

My email is meredith@meredithswift.org

My Instagram is @meredithswiftchristianauthor

ACKNOWLEDGEMENTS AND THANKS

First and foremost, I acknowledge and thank my Lord Jesus Christ for saving me and setting me free. I thank Him for His unfailing love, support, and strength and I pray that He is honoured and glorified through this book.

A huge and heartfelt thank you to all the parents who contributed to this book. I have no doubt that your willingness to share your story will be of help to others who are journeying the same road that you are on.

Over the years there have been many teachers, teacher aides, therapists, support co-ordinators and support workers who have come alongside my family to help, nurture, encourage, and give of their time and expertise. Each one of you has made our journey that little bit easier. Each one of you has contributed to helping my beautiful daughter blossom, with your love and acceptance and willingness to help Sarah grow in her potential. A huge and heartfelt thank you to: Robyn, Jenny, Sharon, Chris, Angie, Carol, Lisa, Rachel, Sarah, Clare, Jewelann, Erica, Megan, Josie, Bonnie, Jean, Liz, Melissa, Helen, Robyn, Yvonne, Sheree, Josh, Zach, Karl, Lachlan, Tali, Wendy, Patty, Jessie, Joyce-Lyn, Ann, Melanie, Lu, Emma, Teisjv, Taylah, Tanya, Jo, Cherie, Maree, Ella, Chloe, Anna, Theresa and Bree.

Thank you to my wonderful launch team for their support, encouragement, and enthusiasm during the publication of this book.

I have been blessed with a loving family, a wonderful group of friends and a precious church family and I thank God every day for all of you.

Last but not least, my thanks to **YOU** for reading my book! I pray that you have found it to be a blessing.

www.ingramcontent.com/pod-product-compliance
Lightning Source LLC
Chambersburg PA
CBHW050305010526
44107CB00055B/2113